the **NO-NONSENSE** guide to

WOMEN'S RIGHTS

Nikki van der Gaag

'Publishers have created lists of short books that discuss the questions that your average [electoral] candidate will only ever touch if armed with a slogan and a soundbite. Together [such books] hint at a resurgence of the grand educational tradition... Closest to the hot headline issues are *The No-Nonsense Guides*. These target those topics that a large army of voters care about, but that politicos evade. Arguments, figures and documents combine to prove that good journalism is far too important to be left to (most) journalists.'

Boyd Tonkin,
The Independent,
London

The No-Nonsense Guide to Women's Rights
First published in the UK by
New Internationalist™ Publications Ltd
Oxford OX4 1BW, UK
www.newint.org
New Internationalist is a registered trade mark.

In association with
Verso
6 Meard Street,
London
W1F 0EG
www.versobooks.com

Cover image: Gabe Palmer/Corbis

Design by New Internationalist Publications Ltd

Typeset by Avocet Typeset, Chilton, Aylesbury, Bucks
Printed by TJ International Ltd, Padstow, Cornwall, UK.

British Library Cataloguing-in-Publication Data.
A catalogue record for this book is available from the British Library.

Library of Congress Cataloguing-in-Publication Data.
A catalogue for this book is available from the Library of Congress.

ISBN 1-84467-502-5

the **NO-NONSENSE** guide to

WOMEN'S RIGHTS
Nikki van der Gaag

VERSO

About the author
Nikki van der Gaag is a feminist and a freelance writer, journalist and editor on development issues. Most recently editorial director at the Panos Institute and co-editor with *New Internationalist*, she has written a number of books, magazines and articles on women and on gender.

Acknowledgements
With thanks to Ines Smyth, Mari Marcel Thekaekara, Tina Wallace and Troth Wells for their insightful comments, to Nawal el Saadawi, and to the many women around the world whose humor and determination have inspired this book.

To my parents Mary and Gerth. Thanks also to my children, Rosa and George, and to my partner Chris for his unfailing support.

Other titles in the series
The No-Nonsense Guide to Globalization
The No-Nonsense Guide to Fair Trade
The No-Nonsense Guide to Climate Change
The No-Nonsense Guide to International Migration
The No-Nonsense Guide to Sexual Diversity
The No-Nonsense Guide to World History
The No-Nonsense Guide to Democracy
The No-Nonsense Guide to Class, Caste and Hierarchies
The No-Nonsense Guide to the Arms Trade
The No-Nonsense Guide to International Development
The No-Nonsense Guide to Indigenous Peoples
The No-Nonsense Guide to Terrorism
The No-Nonsense Guide to HIV/AIDS
The No-Nonsense Guide to World Poverty
The No-Nonsense Guide to Islam
The No-Nonsense Guide to Global Media

Foreword

DURING THE LAST decades feminist movements in the West and the East, in the North and the South, have witnessed a serious backlash. This applies also to the feminist movement in the United States. Young girls and women under the influence of the educational system and media have abandoned the struggle which their mothers and grandmothers began in defense of women's rights. Books have been written by American women who extol the virtues of motherhood and enjoin women to revert to their natural functions, namely rearing their children and caring for their husbands and family.

Some of these books have been translated into Arabic in recent years and have met with enthusiastic support from the authorities and from intellectuals, both men and women, who move in their circles. They have showered praise on these 'new' American women writers who have returned to the family, to the virtues and morality undermined by the feminist movements of so-called women's liberation, which spread to many countries during the middle of the 20th century.

Language is often used against women and the poor in every country, especially in our countries, the so-called 'South'. Today the word 'liberation' means military and economic occupation in Iraq and Afghanistan. The word 'peace' means war, and 'terror' means the massacre of Palestinian women and children under Israeli occupation. The word 'development' means neo-colonialism, robbing people's economic and intellectual riches in Africa, Asia and Latin America.

We need to unveil the words used by global and local governments, by their media and education. Women and the poor, in almost all countries, in the South and the North – but especially in the South – are subjected to a capitalist masculine system based on power and double standards in all domains of life, economic, political, sexual, religious and psychological; at the global, national, family and personal level.

Poor women and children suffer most in this unjust world. They are the first to die in war. They are the first to be dismissed from paid work in any economic crisis. They are the first to die of hunger or poverty. Of the two billion people suffering poverty, 70 per cent are women. Two-thirds of illiterate adults are women. The gender gap is increasing in all areas and there's a growing backlash against women's rights in the South and the North. Women's employment rates have been declining steadily in most countries. Women are obliged to be isolated or veiled for religious reasons, or to expose their bodies for commercial profit. Women's make-up, earrings, high heels, submissive smiles are back. Feminine is good, feminism is evil.

'Family Values' are back in fashion. New laws or family codes have emerged in some countries to give men more power over women and to emphasize traditional gender roles.

The capitalist masculine system benefits a small upper-class group of business and top governmental men and women. Power and money work together to exploit the majority of people, especially poor women and their children.

Nikki van der Gaag's book is a refreshing and enjoyable encounter with her. In it she has made a special effort to correct many of the misconceptions and biases related to the feminist movement, to link the liberation of women who constitute half of society to the liberation of men, and to the dispossessed majority living on the earth.

Nawal El Saadawi
Novelist, Writer
Cairo

the NO-NONSENSE guide to

WOMEN'S RIGHTS

CONTENTS

the **NO-NONSENSE** guide to

WOMEN'S RIGHTS

IT IS 1983. I receive a phone call in my flat in Brixton, south London.

'You know you volunteered to have someone to stay for the Third World women's conference? Well, Nawal El Sadaawi is about to call you from the airport...'

I rush around tidying up. It is cold and we don't have much space. I hadn't expected to have a famous Egyptian feminist to stay. What will she think of the basement flat? How long will she stay? What will I say to her?

In the event, Nawal and her husband Sherif stayed two weeks and every minute was an adventure. Nawal was larger than life and bursting with energy and optimism; Sherif was quiet, intelligent and determined.

It was still the height of the women's movement and I was active in a maelstrom of women's groups and political activities.

I remember one event in particular. The conference that Nawal was to speak at was a big affair. When she and I turned up (no men allowed) she was ushered in and I was sent to the back of the queue. Black and Third World women were to go in first, to reverse the usual order of things. White women had to wait. I was fine about this. Nawal was furious. She insisted that I follow her in and I crept shamefacedly into the gallery – the only white face on the block.

It was one example of the places that women were exploring; how to reverse the usual order of things, to put last first and first last. This was part of the impetus for women-only groups as well. Because in those days women could hardly get a word in edgeways if men were there, women needed their own space. And sometimes pro-woman meant anti-men.

As a result, women all over the world were making huge leaps forward. Feminism was fashionable. Women's rights were on the global agenda. Women's Studies were all the rage. Women led campaigns against sexist advertising, for equal pay, against rape and domestic violence, and marched for abortion. Women's groups mushroomed. There were international women's conferences in Mexico, Nairobi and Beijing. There was strength – and excitement – in numbers for women organizing all over the world.

A woman laborer from India's Self-Employed Women's Association (SEWA) summed up that feeling: 'Until we became organized as a SEWA co-operative, the middlemen could cheat us. But now I can negotiate with them as the representative of our co-operative and as an elected member of our local council. One day near the bus stop I heard a couple of men saying: "There's the woman who is giving us all this trouble. Shall we beat her up?" I told them: "Go ahead and try it. I have 40,000 women behind me!"'[1]

Today, women's issues are no longer headline news, and the excitement of being part of an international women's movement has gone. Women have won their rights, it seems, and it is time to move on. Feminism is past its sell-by date, according to a report from Britain's Equal Opportunities Commission: 'Feminism and the fight for sexual equality are seen by the public as outmoded concepts which are failing to address the strains of modern lives.'

But is this true? While there can be no doubt that there have been huge improvements for many women, particularly in terms of the law, the majority of women in the world continue to live in poverty and oppression. The difference is that what were once collective struggles have become individual sorrows, as women deal with work, childcare or simply fetching water for the family – alone.

And most men have changed very little, although some have been allies in the fight for women's rights.

Now the gains women have made are under threat from the religious establishment in a number of countries – from the American Christian Right, led by President George W Bush, and from Islamic and other fundamentalist movements.

In May 2001 Nawal El Sadaawi became one of their targets. A case was brought against her in Egypt saying that, after 37 years, she should be divorced from Sherif for not being a true Muslim.

The couple mobilized international opinion – and are still married.

People like Nawal and Sherif, and those who supported them, are working together, seeing clearly the links between women's rights and the rights of all oppressed groups and peoples.

And Nawal remains eternally optimistic. In a speech in Cairo in November 2002 she praised the 'collective global and local resistance' that she believed 'is increasing in power and scope day after day. It is the source of our hope in the future, the creative human effort of people who dream of a world where they can live in justice and freedom and peace.'[2]

I hope she is right.

Nikki van der Gaag
Oxford

1 World Summit for Social Development and beyond, Geneva, June 2000, quoted in *World Development Report 2000/2001 – Attacking Poverty*.
2 http://www.nawalsaadawi.net/articlesnawal/bornexile.htm

1 The new war on women

The advances women have made over the last 20 years cannot hide the fact that for millions of women life is still very grim. And now even the gains that have been made are under threat.

'*The repression of women [is] everywhere and always wrong.*'
George W Bush[1]

WOMEN'S RIGHTS, IN theory at least, are well established. This is partly due to the heritage of feminism; many years of pressure from women's groups and organizations on the international establishment has put 'gender equality' firmly on the global agenda. It has had some tangible results and, importantly, women themselves are more aware of their rights.

Changes for the better

- More women are working – since 1980 the growth in women's labor force has been substantially higher than that of men in every region of the world except Africa.
- More girls are being educated – the gap between boys' and girls' enrollments has narrowed. In Africa the number of illiterate women has fallen by 6.4 per cent in the last 10 years.
- Women are living longer – average life expectancy in developing countries, 53.7 years in 1970, rose to 62.9 years in 1992.
- Women are having fewer children – 50 per cent of women now have access to modern contraceptives.
- There are more women in politics – especially at grassroots levels. In 22 countries women represent more than 25 per cent of those in government.
- Legislation, from international to local, is recognizing that women's rights need to be protected.
- There are more liberal marriage laws in some countries: in the North the average age of marriage is going up.
- Lesbian women in some countries have more rights than they did before – 19 Northern countries now have some legislation recognizing same-sex relationships.
- Female genital cutting has been outlawed in six African countries. ∎

But there is another side to the story. Of 1.3 billion people living in poverty, 70 per cent are women. Two-thirds of illiterate adults are women. In parts of the North the gender gap in earnings persists – for example, the average British woman earns 63 per cent of the wages of the average man.[2] Women's share of decision-making positions reached 30 per cent in only 28 countries in the 1990s.

In many countries there has been a growing 'back-lash' against the gains women have made.[3] Sometimes this is economic (see Chapter 4): for example, in the countries of the former Soviet Union, the end of the Cold War and the advent of the free market have also meant the end of a range of benefits for women – maternity pay, free healthcare and education – driving many back into poverty.

Sometimes the backlash is cultural or religious: the rise of religious conservatism worldwide resulted in heightened legal and social restrictions on women in 25 countries between the late 1990s and 2002. These countries include Algeria, Niger, Nigeria, Sudan, Democratic Republic of Congo, Gabon, Uganda, Somalia, Swaziland, Qatar, Yemen, Iran, Pakistan, Kuwait, Saudi Arabia, Egypt, Turkey, Jordan, Afghanistan, India, Bangladesh, Thailand, Malaysia, Brunei and the United States.[4]

In the Muslim world, fundamentalists' narrow inter-pretations of the Qur'an amount to an attack on women's rights. 'In any situation where religious fundamentalism is on the rise it will always impact on women because at the heart of the religious funda-mentalist agenda is the control of women, of repro-ductive rights and of the family,' says Pragna Patel of Southall Black Sisters in Britain.[5]

Beliefs and practices are being dredged up from the past by fundamentalists and recast, sometimes in countries where they were never common practice. In Sri Lanka, for example, some groups demanded the introduction of female genital cutting (FGC, sometimes known as female genital mutilation) as an 'Islamic duty', despite the fact that no-one in Sri Lanka had ever practiced FGC and that it has nothing to do with Islam.

In Pakistan there were attempts to import a North African interpretation of religious law in which a woman always remains a minor and is never able to enter into a contract in her own right. This is part of Algerian and Moroccan law but had never been part of religious practice in Pakistan.

In Algeria, *muta'a* marriage is being reintroduced in fundamentalist military camps. This is a 'temporary' marriage which can be entered into for years, months or just days. It should require both parties' consent. It is a Shi'a practice and had never been used in Algeria until fundamentalist men wanted to make their rape of young women in villages they raided legitimate. [6]

Karma Nabulsi, a politics research fellow at Oxford University in Britain, says: 'When the political élites face battles with the Islamists, all of their opponents' arguments are being cast as "We want to get rid of the West", and women's rights are part of that.'

This restriction of women's rights, as part of an anti-West agenda, is not confined to the Muslim world.

In Uganda, which has a positive record on women's rights, an amendment to the Land Act which would have given married women the right to own land was rejected by President Museveni on the grounds that he wanted to save the world from the mistakes of the West. 'It is like telling the Karimojong [nomadic herders] that Parliament had passed a Bill allowing women to share cows,' he said. 'There will be a civil war.' [7] The Women of Uganda network says: 'His ideological stance is trapped in a 1960s time-warp, and the questions he raises on gender are out of step with what is now the general understanding of what constitutes gender issues. The President's analysis of issues is contradictory in that while he is loathsome of

Western values, he projects a social evolution that is determinedly Western and capitalist.'[8]

Suddenly, women's rights have become an import, along with Coca-Cola, Levi jeans and pornography. The irony is that a huge amount of the thinking and the pushing through of women's issues over the last 10 or 20 years has come from women in the countries of the South, who saw the inequalities they lived with and decided to do something about them. 'The notion that feminism is Western is still bandied about by those ignorant of history or who perhaps more will-fully employ it in a delegitimizing way,' says scholar Margot Badran. 'Feminism, however, is a plant that only grows in its own soil'.[9]

For some Muslim women, veiling has become part of a wider statement against the West. Where 25 years ago liberation meant throwing off the *hijab* [veil], today women who would never have worn the veil before are doing so in large numbers.

The events of 11 September 2001 exacerbated this trend, and meant that many people were forced to choose specific identities that separated them into narrow groupings – 'with us' or 'against us', Muslim or Christian, black or white.

This had a number of direct consequences for women, particularly black women, as Pragna Patel notes: 'September 11 affected us in a way that we had never felt before in the sense that walking down the street you felt very conscious about being different... it felt very personal. People were looking at you as if to say "We don't trust you". "We don't want you here."'

It also ran counter to the ways that women had been successfully working together: 'One of the success stories of Asian women organizing is that they have crossed the divides of racial identity, religion and culture so the struggles have benefited all and brought these communities together... But [September 11] has affected all groups. You will no longer hear: "This is an Asian woman talking about issues that affect Asian communities." You will hear: "This is a Muslim woman talking about Muslim communities."'[10]

In Britain this climate of fear, and the racism that comes with it, have meant negative public attitudes towards asylum-seekers just when they most need refuge. For women, claiming refuge on the basis of what is legally known as 'gender persecution' has become more difficult – an irony at a time when

Turning into a Muslim

I was at a conference in Birmingham which I went into as normal, my usual mixed-up self, full of odd thoughts and random worries. As that day, 11 September, unfolded, I turned into a Muslim. Of course I was born a Muslim in Iran, I grew up as one under the Shah in the 1950s and 1960s, but I had never really thought about it, it wasn't an issue, just there in the background. But after that conference I took a taxi back to the station. The driver was a Muslim, and when he realized I was one as well, he slowed right down. He asked me what we could do, as Muslims, about this terrible event, and about our own position. We progressed across that city at around ten miles an hour – and talked and talked.

I am a scholar, a teacher, somebody who engages in arguments, in dialogue, reasoned debate. For the first time, I was someone who had started getting hate mail. It came from people who had just seen that I was on TV or on the radio, without knowing what I had said beyond maybe a sound bite. Thus I was categorized as Muslim, troublesome, by people who I had never met and who had never heard what I have to say in any depth. I would get these vile postcards, and I remember my head of department scribbling on one of them: 'We don't all think like this, my dear!'

Now, there have been notions and proposals about solidarity kicking around in the Muslim community for years. People talked about it, but, *in extremis*, it began to make a sort of sense. I had not made a habit of announcing my identity, it was not relevant, but as that period unfolded, I felt I no longer had any choice. For years I had been denouncing the policies and practice of places like Saudi Arabia, but suddenly there were all sorts of issues on which I felt it inappropriate to voice criticisms. Those times didn't seem the right time.

It has also meant I found myself in meetings alongside all sorts of strange bedfellows, people who I had, in some cases, previously refused to be in the same room with. I chaired meetings where I found myself in some degree of sympathy with fundamentalists there. Why was that? Because we had been categorized as Muslim terrorists together by the outside world.

Maybe it is because I am used to working within liberal academia, where it is less of an issue than in other harsher places where Muslims are trying to make themselves invisible, but all of this has brought out the Muslim in me, an attitude of 'I will face you all'. I object to being cowed. ∎

Haleh Afshar is professor of Middle Eastern politics at the University of York.

The Guardian, 11 September 2002.

Western governments are trumpeting the cause of women in other countries.

The backlash is also a moral one. Family values are back in fashion. Rick Santorum, the third-highest ranking Republican in the US Senate under the Bush administration, said 'feminists and liberals' are 'hurting American families'. Major women's rights organizations in the US released a scorecard rating the Bush administration on key issues affecting women internationally: it merited a 'B+' for rhetoric and an 'F' for reality.[11]

For despite its pro-woman rhetoric and its championing of women's rights abroad, in the US the Bush administration has slashed social programs for single mothers, attacked affirmative action for women, cut funds to any organizations – national or international – that were seen to be supporting abortion, tied large chunks of HIV and AIDS funding to programs that promoted sexual abstinence, and appointed right-wing radicals with conservative views on women to powerful positions.

The US National Organization of Women said: 'Piece by piece, Bush is tearing down the progress women and other disenfranchised groups have made over the last 35 years, ensuring that rich white males and giant corporations will rule the US for generations to come.'

What the Bush Administration has done is not new; it is part of a slow drip-drip wearing away the gains that women have made. The new administrations in Iraq and Afghanistan have seen few women in positions of power. In Afghanistan women have been largely excluded from the rebuilding of their country, despite US Secretary of State Colin Powell's fine words: 'The recovery of Afghanistan must entail the restoration of the rights of Afghan women. Indeed, it will not be possible without them. The rights of the women of Afghanistan will not be negotiable.'[12] The new Ministry of Women's Affairs did not receive

The truth about George W and women's rights

- Funds to organizations that support abortion in any way were withdrawn, as was $34 million in congressionally allotted aid to the United Nations Population Fund; $3 million for the World Health Organization's reproductive-health program was frozen; UN conferences have been used to push a pro-life agenda. (see Chapter 2 for more details)
- In June 2003 Congress outlawed a form of late termination in the US – the most significant restriction on abortion since it was legalized in 1973.
- Bush supported a policy that prohibited military women serving abroad, and their dependents, from obtaining safe medical abortions at military hospitals, even if they paid.
- In the 2002 budget Bush proposed eliminating required contraceptive coverage for female federal employees and federal employees' dependents. Andrea Brooks, director of the women's and fair-practices department at the American Federation of Government Employees, called the proposal 'extremely discriminatory'.
- Attorney General John Ashcroft wanted to issue new gender-persecution regulations limiting battered immigrant women seeking asylum.
- The White House Office for Women's Initiatives and Outreach was closed on 19 January 2001. It had been set up under Clinton as a conduit for women's political concerns. ■

www.thetruthaboutgeorge.com/women/index.html
http://washingtonpost.com/wp-dyn/articles/A8599-2001Mar28.html

enough funding to carry out effective work. And one of just two women ministers, Sima Samar, resigned after a campaign of vilification.

Women's rights, men's rights
In the West some men – and women – feel strongly that women's rights are only being granted at the expense of men's rights. The Men's Movement in Britain is at the strident end of this:

'We regard the assertion that women are disadvantaged as The Big Lie of our time. And feminism is based on The Big Lie. There can be no greater folly

Profile: Sima Samar

Sima Samar was born in Afghanistan in February 1957. She belongs to the Hazara minority, one of the most persecuted in the country, comprising around 17 per cent of the population. At 18 she married, and trained as a doctor. In 1982 she became the first Hazara woman to get a degree in medicine from Kabul University.

At that time about 30 per cent of civil servants and 70 per cent of teachers were women. When Samar was growing up, Afghan women could go to school, have jobs, dress how they liked and earn wages equal to men's. They were allowed to vote and held political office. Then the Russians invaded, and she helped the anti-Soviet resistance movement, the *mujahideen*. In 1984 her husband was arrested and she fled to Pakistan with her young son. She worked as a doctor in a refugee camp in Quetta, where thousands of refugees from Afghanistan lived in squalid conditions. She never heard from her husband again.

In 1989 she opened her first hospital for women in Quetta. Now, through her nonprofit Shuhada Organization, she runs an additional four hospitals and ten clinics in Afghanistan, and rural schools for 22,000 girls and boys. Another 1,000 children attend her school in Quetta.

In December 2002, with the Taliban gone and the advent of the new government under Hamid Karzai, Samar was invited back to the country she had left nearly 20 years earlier and offered the post of Deputy Prime Minister and Minister for Women's Affairs. What she wanted for women, she said, was simply what they had before the Taliban came to power. 'I want rights for women on all levels, in the political and social sectors, in everything – right to vote, right to be elected, right to work everywhere.'

But her outspokenness, it seems, won her few friends, and soon she was accused of 'blasphemy' and of being 'Afghanistan's Salman Rushdie'. After six months in the job she resigned, leaving only one other woman – Health Minister Suhaila Siddiqa – in the Afghan cabinet. ∎

or degeneracy than to provide further support, via Ministers for Women etc, to the most privileged group in our society – women – while denying the disadvantaged, suppressed and persecuted group – men – any representation at all. Feminism is about women getting something for nothing. The question of whether "feminism has gone too far" is perhaps less important than "why feminism was established at all".

Feminism is an aberration, like Nazism and communism – a blight on our society.'[13]

They are not the only ones to see feminism, and the gains women have made, in this light. A South African study suggests that recently reported high levels of violence against women may be partly fueled by male backlash against the progress women have made.[14] Researchers have referred to this as 'neopatriarchy' – a new attempt to exert male authority, in this case through a culture of sexual violence.[15]

Fighting back

But women are not just submitting passively to these assaults. In many Muslim countries they are arguing for the right to define what it means to be Muslim. Saad Hamid, a lawyer advising the Palestinian women's legal-reform movement in Gaza, says that many in the Arab world are searching for avenues to advance women's rights within the context of Islam. 'Solutions to 90 per cent of the problems exist within

---

Wispy scarves: women in Iran

In Iran, where women have been educated since separate education for girls and boys was introduced after the 1979 revolution, there is another quiet revolution going on. Girls are wearing wispy colored scarves and their long coats are getting shorter. The authorities are trying to fight back; they issued an order in May 2003 calling for an end to the manufacture and sale of transparent scarves and tight-fitting coats. 'It's nonsense,' says Mitra, a young woman who works at the cosmetic counter of a shop. 'Everyone should have the right to wear what they want.' Reformist Member of Parliament Elahe Kolaee said that if they couldn't buy the clothes they wanted, women would make their own. It is not just clothes that are changing. One in three marriages in Tehran now ends in divorce. Women are working as lawyers, doctors and managers. And once 'a woman steps out onto the street, she cannot be a traditional woman any more,' says Ebadi. ∎

Adapted from Dan de Luce, 'The Audrey look is very in and the mood is defiant', *The Guardian*, 12 June 2003.

Islam if you want to find them,' says Hamid. 'What we're trying to do is show that there are different schools of Islamic jurisprudence. Saying I know nothing about it, and I want to banish it and have purely secular laws, that's ridiculous.'[16]

Writer Leila Ahmed noted in her novel *A Border Passage*: 'Generations of astute, thoughtful women listening to the Qur'an understood perfectly well its essential themes and its faith. And looking around them, they understood perfectly well, too, what a travesty men had made of it.' 'My problem is not with Islam, it is with the culture of patriarchy,' says Iranian human-rights lawyer Shirin Ebadi.

Patriarchy – a system based on male power – has been challenged all over the world. There is a real sense that women have not just made practical steps forward, but at all levels they have gained in confidence as a result of the changes wrested from those in power over the last 10 years. This is by no means a

---

Shirin Ebadi

She is the first Muslim woman and the first Iranian to win the Nobel Peace Prize. A lawyer and activist, she has fallen foul of her country's conservative clerics, and been threatened and imprisoned.

Born in 1947, she served under the Shah as one of Iran's first female judges, but had to step down after the 1979 revolution introduced the rule of conservative clerics, who said that women could not be judges. That interpretation of Shari'a law is now being questioned and some religious leaders are calling for their reinstatement.

Ebadi supports women's rights, and those of children and refugees, and has been involved in a number of controversial legal cases as a result. She strongly defends freedom of speech, campaigns for peaceful and democratic solutions to her country's problems, and promotes new thinking on Islam.

Receiving the prize in October 2003, she told a press conference that her prize 'belongs to all people who work for human rights in Iran'.

'As a lawyer, judge, lecturer, writer and activist, she has spoken out clearly and strongly in her country, Iran, and far beyond its borders,' said the Awards Committee. ■

Northern phenomenon alone – the march towards equality for women has had little to do with how 'developed' a country is, and more to do with political will, cultural change and the commitment of society at large to women's rights. This is nothing new: it can be seen from earliest times.

Women's rights 900 BC – 2001

A snapshot of history shows that women have always struggled for their rights, and that progress is not a straight line; many societies where women are most repressed today were the most enlightened in the past. History shows us that rights can be won – and they can also be taken away. These are some landmarks on the road that women have been struggling along for centuries.

900 BC In ancient Sumer (Iraq), Egypt and Japan, adult women can own property, play active roles in the marketplace and even be clerics. In pre-colonial Latin America, some native cultures practice what anthropologists call 'gender parallelism' valuing equally the distinct and overlapping tasks performed by men and women. The agrarian societies that follow tend to be less egalitarian.

1400s Trade brings new status to women in some countries. In Nigeria, among the Igbo, a wealthy woman can buy a 'wife' to work with her and Yoruba women elect their own female representatives to protect their trading interests.

1776 During the French Revolution working women march on Versailles to demand bread. In 1791 this inspires French playwright Olympe de Gouges to issue the *Declaration of the Rights of Woman and the Female Citizen.* She is executed by guillotine when demands for women's rights are rejected.

1792 In Britain Mary Wollstonecraft rejects conventional family authority, believes in female education, and bears a child out of wedlock. She writes *A Vindication of the Rights of Woman* which becomes a catalyst for subsequent feminist thinking.

1848 The world's first women's rights convention (with men as well as women) is held in Seneca Falls, New York, setting the agenda for the movement.

1850s In Brazil, women's urban newspapers like *O Jornal das Senhoras* (Ladies' Journal) complain that marriage is 'an unbearable tyranny' and women deserve 'a just enjoyment of their rights'.

1861 In Russia the emancipation of serfs raises women's expectations of equality.

1880-1890 The Japanese women's movement is founded. Kishida Toshiko is jailed for a week after calling for women's horizons to be 'as large and free as the world itself'. The Government eventually bans women's political participation.

1893 New Zealand becomes the first country to give women the vote.

1896 In the US the National Association of Colored Women, founded by Margaret Murray Washington, unites Black women's organizations, with Mary Church Terrell its first president. The NACW becomes a major vehicle for reform during the next 40 years.

1890-1923 Islam is used to justify the education of women. In 1923 Huda Sha'rawawi founds the Egyptian Feminist Union. Women are at the forefront of the battle for independence from the British.

1911 Socialists observe 8 March as a day to honor the women who organized strikes for better working conditions. In Mexico Jovita and Soledad Pena organize *La Liga Femenil Mexicanista* (League of Mexican Feminists).

1913 In South Africa traditional women's organizations such as Manyano act as savings clubs for poor women. They are also at the forefront of the fight against apartheid.

1920 In the US, African American women meet to

discuss how they can 'stand side by side with women of the white race and work for the full emancipation of all women'(Lugenia Burns Hope).

1926 In Turkey, as part of his program for modernization, Kamal Ataturk abolishes polygamy, makes schools and universities coeducational, gives women political rights and recognizes the equal rights of women in divorce, custody and inheritance.

1929 The 'women's war' in Nigeria is a response among Igbo women's trading networks to the planned imposition by the British rulers of a new tax on women's property. The British put down the revolt by firing into the crowd, killing 50 women and injuring 50.

1941 In the US almost seven million women take jobs during the war; two million as industrial 'Rosie the Riveters' and 400,000 joining the military.

1947 Gandhi expresses strong opposition to male domination of women, and India's first Prime Minister, Jawaharlal Nehru, calls for equal educational and work opportunities for women and men. Nationalists adopt the slogan: 'India cannot be free until its women are free and women cannot be free until India is free.' The 1947 Constitution guarantees equality between the sexes.

1948 In Egypt, Doria Shafik forms the Daughters of the Nile Union. In 1951 she organizes an invasion of the Egyptian parliament by women and in 1953 creates a women's political party that is then suppressed by the government.

1959 In eastern Nigeria 2,000 women protest their declining status by occupying and setting fire to a market. They negotiate a resolution that eliminates all foreign courts and schools and expels all foreigners in the area.

1977 Argentinean women form the 'Mothers of the Plaza de Mayo' to defy the murderous military junta that seized power from President Isabel Peron of Argentina.

1975-2001 The birth and growth of the feminist movement. First international women's conference in Mexico, launching the United Nations Decade for Women and the formation of women's groups all over the world, including feminist newspapers, student organizations, professional women and lesbian feminists. Followed by conferences in Copenhagen (1980), Nairobi (1985) and Beijing (1995). Women's rights become enshrined in law in many countries.

1 From the *New York Times*, quoted in *The Guardian,* Katharine Viner, 21 September 21, 2002. **2** Jamie Doward and Tom Reilly, 'Shameful pay makes British women worst off in Europe', *The Observer*, 12 October 2003. **3** Susan Faludi, *Backlash; the Undeclared War against Women*, Chatto and Windus, 1991. **4** Joni Seager, *The Atlas of Women*, The Women's Press, 2003. **5** *Trouble and Strife* 43, Summer 2002. **6** Above examples from an interview with Marieme Helie Lucas of Women Living Under Muslim Laws in *Trouble and Strife* 43, Summer 2002. **7** *The East African*, 13 March 2000. **8** http://www.wougnet.org/Alerts/drbresponseEK.html **9** http://weekly. ahram.org.eg/2002/569/cu1.htm **10** *Trouble and Strife* 43, Summer 2002. **11** www.womensissues.about.com **12** Remarks at the Eisenhower Executive Office Building, Washington, DC. **13** http://www.ukmm.org.uk/ **14** N Anderson et al, *Beyond Victims and Villains: The Culture of Sexual Violence in South Johannesburg*, Community Information and Transparency Foundation (CIET) Africa, 2000. **15** *Beyond victims and villains: addressing sexual violence in the education sector,* Panos, 2003. **16** Karma Nabulsi and Saad Hamid are quoted in www.christiansciencemonitor.org

2 Birth and death

From birth to death women still face unnecessary dangers to their health, just because they are women. Female fetuses are aborted because they are female, hundreds of thousands of women die in childbirth, and increasing numbers live in the shadow of the HIV/AIDS epidemic.

'Reproductive rights rest on the recognition of the basic right of all couples and individuals to decide freely and responsibly the number, spacing and timing of their children and to have the information and means to do so, and the right to attain the highest standards of sexual and reproductive health.'

World Health Organization[1]

A dangerous business

BECOMING A MOTHER is still a dangerous business. Every day more than 1,500 women die from preventable complications arising from pregnancy and birth – that is over half a million women a year.[2] Many millions more suffer illness and ill-health, often long-term, as a result of giving birth.

Maternal deaths are also one of the most obvious indicators of the widening gap between rich and poor. Ninety-nine per cent of deaths occur in the countries of the South. African women are 175 times more likely to die in childbirth than women in the North. In the year 2000, 13 developing countries accounted for 70 per cent of all maternal deaths. The highest number occurred in India where 136,000 women died, followed by Nigeria where there were 37,000 deaths.[3]

Poor women and those from minority groups in the North are also more at risk than their richer sisters – in the US, five white women die for every 100,000 births, but the figures rise to 10 if you are a Hispanic woman, 12 if you are Native American and 20 if you are African-American.[4]

So why are so many women still dying in the process of becoming mothers? Poverty is one simple answer. If you are poor you are more likely to die giving birth than if you are rich. Poor women, and women in poor countries, often have neither the resources nor the knowledge to prevent such deaths. Often they also have little access to clinics or hospitals, including maternity services and ante-natal care.

Resources, or the lack of them, provide another part of the answer. In a study of 49 developing countries almost half the maternal-health services were judged to be so poorly resourced that they could not carry out one or more of the lifesaving procedures they were meant to offer.

This comes down to priorities. The World Bank has estimated that the financial cost of basic maternal health services in developing countries is $2 per person per year.

The tragedy is that almost all maternal deaths are preventable. The main medical cause of maternal death is severe bleeding. The others are infection, unsafe abortion and eclampsia (convulsions, or seizures, during or immediately after pregnancy). Anemia also poses a risk to pregnant women – in Asia 60 per cent are anemic, in Africa 52 per cent, in Latin

America 39 per cent, in Europe and the US 17 per cent. Basic health facilities and medicines would save nearly all of these lives. But, it seems, women's health is not high on the global agenda – or on national agendas.

Preventable deaths

In one Indonesian study 60 per cent of maternal deaths involved serious haemorrhage. This is a description of one such birth:

'At 4 am she began to experience labor pains... her husband called the traditional birth attendant three hours later. [By the evening] the baby was still not coming. [The traditional birth attendant] decided to call the midwife, but the midwife was absent... At 9 am the next morning the baby emerged.

The midwife arrived a few minutes later... The placenta was still attached to the roof of the womb... As they struggled to remove the placenta, bleeding continued and five or six kain (a piece of cloth used to absorb the blood and staunch the flow) were soon filled.

By 9.30 pm the placenta was out, but the bleeding continued. The midwife was beginning to panic and urged the family to take her to the hospital. They hesitated, replying that they didn't have the money to pay the costs, but the midwife insisted...

They obtained a car... By 11 pm they were checking [the woman] into the emergency ward.

The hospital midwife described later how blood was spurting from the vagina. 'The [woman] was unconscious and the doctor realized she would need blood immediately for an operation... There was no fresh blood available. At midnight the woman died.' ∎

M B Iskandar, B Utomo, T Hull, NG Dharmaputra, Y Azwar, *Unravelling the mysteries of maternal death in West Java: Re-examining the witnesses*, Center for Health Research, Research Institute, University of Indonesia, 1996, quoted in Judy Mirsky, *Birth rights: new approaches to safe motherhood*, Panos Institute, 2001.

Teenage mothers

The younger you are, the more risky pregnancy is – girls aged 10 to 14 are five times more likely to die in pregnancy or childbirth than women in their early twenties. Their bodies are not yet fully grown, their hips too small for childbirth. They face an added risk of malnutrition, anemia, injury and infection. And yet approximately 15 million adolescent girls give birth each year, more than 10 per cent of all births worldwide. Many young women giving birth too early are afflicted with obstetric fistulae; the result of trauma during childbirth. Fistula is a tear in the birth canal, either into the rectum or urethra, that constantly leaks bodily wastes. The sufferer is usually ostracized, abandoned and shamed. Fistulae continue to strike 50,000 to 100,000 adolescent girls and women in developing countries each year.[5]

A very high proportion of teenage pregnancies are unwanted. Every year teenagers seek about four million abortions.

So why are young girls having babies? In some countries religious and cultural traditions insist on early marriage. Every year 82 million young women between the ages of 10 and 17 are married. More than 50 countries allow marriage at 16 or younger, and seven allow it as young as 12. In sub-Saharan Africa more than 50 per cent of women give birth before the age of 20. And in other countries young people are having sex younger and younger – the messages of safe sex and pregnancy prevention are clearly not getting across. In the US, 22 per cent of 15 to 19-year-olds who have sexual intercourse become pregnant.

Fertility and family planning

'A woman's health prospects are transformed if she can decide whether and when she wants to have children,' says Margaret Catley-Carlson, President of the Population Council.[6]

Women are having fewer children than their mothers and grandmothers. In the last 30 years women's use of contraceptives has increased dramatically. More than 50 per cent of the world's women now use modern contraceptive methods.[7] Many more would prefer to be able to plan their pregnancies. But access to modern contraception, medical advice and follow-up is not available to all who want them.

Types of contraception for women

While men remain reluctant to consider sterilization, despite the fact that the operation is a relatively minor one compared to female sterilization, the latter remains the most common form of contraception. Despite the risk of HIV/AIDs, condoms still account for less than 10 per cent of contraceptive methods used.

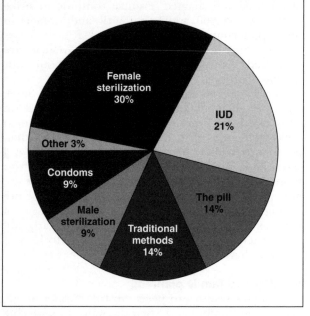

Female sterilization 30%
IUD 21%
Other 3%
Condoms 9%
The pill 14%
Male sterilization 9%
Traditional methods 14%

The Atlas of Women: an economic, social and political survey, Joni Seager, third edition, 2003, The Women's Press

Husbands may prevent their wives from using contraception for a variety of reasons, including the argument that she may become 'promiscuous' if she is freed from worry about having children.

Contraceptive use is uneven, with women in richer countries and urban areas having the best access, while others spend most of their reproductive lives bearing children every year.

Nearly 230 million women – almost one in six women of reproductive age – still need the choice of effective family planning in order to space or limit the size of their families. More than 50 per cent of women in some countries report that they would have preferred to postpone or avoid their most recent birth.[8] With so much rhetoric today about choice, it is interesting to note that a woman's right to choose how many children she wants hardly exists in many parts of the world.

At 30 per cent worldwide, female sterilization remains the most common contraceptive method – in Australia, 38 per cent of women have been sterilized, in Brazil 43 per cent and in El Salvador 60 per cent.

Abuses are common; governments of countries like the US, China and India have imposed sterilization on minority or poor women during the last three decades. Male sterilization is a much simpler operation, but is undergone by only a tiny proportion of men, who feel that it somehow challenges their 'manhood'.

Global pharmaceutical companies have marketed unsafe or experimental contraceptives, particularly to poor women. 'Women still face the dilemma that the safest contraceptives are not the most effective, while the most effective are not necessarily the safest,' says Joni Seager, author of *The Atlas for Women*.

Son preference

'If she has given birth to a son the family will care about her,' says one woman from Nepal. 'But if she has given birth to a baby girl they will neglect her. She has to do [the] operation of family planning after giving a birth to a son. But she cannot do operation until she gives birth to a son. If she gives birth to a girl, she has to continue it till the son is born.'[9]

The global preference for sons over daughters remains marked. In some places this produces demographic distortion – the biological norm is for 95 girls to be born for every 100 boys, but male infants have a higher mortality rate so by early childhood the numbers should be even. In countries including South Korea, India, China, Bangladesh and Pakistan there are now as few as 80 girls per 100 boys. About seven per cent of girls under the age of five are 'missing' in China and Korea, more than four per cent in India and other parts of South Asia.

The availability of genetic testing also means that in some countries it is used to select female fetuses for abortion. In India genetic testing for sex selection is a booming business. Indian gender-detection clinics drew protests from women's groups, especially after the appearance of advertisements suggesting that it was better to 'spend $38 now to terminate a female fetus than $3,800 later on a daughter's dowry'. Far more female than male fetuses are aborted. 'Without such discrimination,' says the World Bank, 'there would be an estimated 60 to 100 million more women in the world.'[10]

Son-preference is not just a Southern phenomenon. Asked how many children he had fathered, the former world heavyweight boxing champion Muhammad Ali told an interviewer: 'One boy and seven mistakes.'[11]

Abortion

An estimated 38 per cent of all pregnancies are unintended.[12] There are around 25 to 30 million legal abortions in the world each year, and another 20 million unsafe, illegal ones; 40,000 women die from the complications that follow.[13] One way of reducing levels of abortion is to prevent unwanted pregnancy by making family-planning services more accessible. In the Central Asian countries of Kazakhstan, Uzbekistan and the Kyrgyz Republic better availability of services and information has increased the use of modern contraception by 30-50 per cent since 1990, and abortion rates have declined by half.[14]

Since the 1980s pressure from women has led to

more liberal abortion laws in some countries. But 25 per cent of the world's women still live in countries where abortion is illegal – or only legal if a woman's life is in danger.

And there has been a backlash in the last 10 years. Rather than a full assault on abortion, the American Right has generally opted for a piecemeal approach, changing a small piece of legislation here and there; enforcing laws which say that women must look at photographs of fetuses before deciding to abort (Texas' deceptively named 'Women's Right to Know' act) or enacting laws which mandate punishment for causing harm to a fetus during a crime, such as rape or burglary (26 states, including California). In South Carolina there is discussion about the construction of a giant fetus on state land. In Oklahoma and Georgia legislators are considering asking women to sign a death warrant before they have an abortion.

'What they are doing is very clandestine,' says Julia Ernst of the Center for Reproductive Rights. 'They are not doing a frontal assault. They are trying to fly under the radar screen, in part not to tip off the American public.' But it amounts to an outright attack on abortion – 'an assault on reproductive rights writ large,' says Ernst.[15] The latest controversy is

---

Anti-abortion backlash

In the US and Canada between 1992 and 2002:

- 7 abortion clinic workers were murdered
- 15 murders were attempted
- 97 arson or bombing attacks were made on abortion clinics
- 272 additional death threats were made
- 443 incidents of stalking workers or patients were reported
- 654 anthrax mail threats were received ■

Joni Seager, *The Atlas of Women*, The Women's Press, third edition, 2003.

over a proposed law which outlaws a form of late termination.

Some go even further. Groups like Operation Rescue have targeted – and even killed – people connected with abortion clinics.

The 'global gag' rule

In 2001 President Bush introduced a policy that disqualifies non-governmental organizations (NGOs) outside the US from receiving US funding if they provide legal abortion services (except in very narrow circumstances), counsel on termination or lobby in favor of legal abortion in their own country. This includes a decision to withhold $34 million in assistance to the UN Population Fund (UNFPA) on the grounds that its programs 'promote' abortion. UNFPA estimates the lost funds will translate into two million more unwanted pregnancies, 800,000 more abortions, 4,700 more dead mothers and 77,000 deaths of children under five.

Congressman Joseph Crowley is among those battling to get the funding reinstated: 'By withholding our contribution to UNFPA, we send a strong message to women in the developing world that we choose not to help.'

In 2003 this policy – known to those who oppose it as the 'global gag rule' – was extended to include a proposed $15 billion fund to combat HIV/AIDS. In a protest letter to Bush, women's groups across the world said:

'We know that integrated sexual and reproductive healthcare saves lives, and that the single most effective strategy to prevent unnecessary deaths is to combine political will, economic resources and sound public-health policies to strengthen and expand access to sexual and reproductive health services. Each and every one of these deaths can be prevented. Yet we watch as the US attempts on every level to undermine such services throughout the world.'[16]

New technologies

The irony here is that although the last quarter of the 20th century saw many women still dying from illegal abortions, it also witnessed several major advances in reproductive medicine. One of the most controversial is the use of assisted reproductive technology (ART) to manage infertility. ART includes treatments like In-vitro Fertilization (IVF) but also surrogacy (where a woman agrees to become pregnant and bear a child for a couple who often pay her) and the freezing of eggs and sperm.

Infertility affects more than 80 million people worldwide, or one in ten couples. Most of these live in the South where infertility services in general, and ART in particular, are not available.[17]

Sexually transmitted diseases

There are 333 million people who contract curable sexually transmitted diseases (excluding AIDS) each year. One third of these are young people under 25. The consequences for women can be very serious and sometimes fatal (cervical cancer, ectopic pregnancy, sepsis). And yet women tend not to seek treatment – partly because the majority of such infections do not have any major symptoms, partly because they fear the stigma attached to having such an infection and may have neither time nor money for healthcare.

HIV/AIDS

Twenty years ago HIV/AIDS was largely a men's disease. But by the end of 2002 women made up half the 42 million people living with the condition. Of the five million new people infected with HIV during that year, half were women. Seventy per cent of people living with HIV/AIDs are in sub-Saharan Africa, of whom women make up 58 per cent. When women die their children are put at risk, even if they do not have the disease. For a girl, the death of her mother increases her chances of dying by 400 per cent.

People living with HIV/AIDS, 2002

In sub-Saharan Africa, North Africa and the Middle East, women now make up more than half of those living with HIV/AIDS. And this percentage continues to increase...

Total number of people and percentage of women

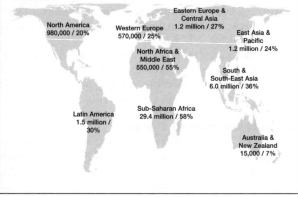

North America
980,000 / 20%

Western Europe
570,000 / 25%

Eastern Europe &
Central Asia
1.2 million / 27%

East Asia &
Pacific
1.2 million / 24%

North Africa &
Middle East
550,000 / 55%

South &
South-East Asia
6.0 million / 36%

Latin America
1.5 million /
30%

Sub-Saharan Africa
29.4 million / 58%

Australia &
New Zealand
15,000 / 7%

So why have the numbers of women with HIV/ AIDS increased so dramatically, especially in Africa?

First, because their physiology is more vulnerable to HIV and other sexually transmitted infections than men's. Reproductive-tract infections, which predispose to HIV infection, are more easily transmitted and less easy to diagnose in women. Vaginal cuts suffered during violent or coerced sex increase the risks.

Second, because women rarely have the power in a relationship to negotiate condom use, or to prevent their husband or partner having relationships with others who may be infected.

Young women in particular are vulnerable. One study estimates that over half the world's population has had unprotected sex by the age of 16.[18] HIV infection rates among African women aged 15-19 in some urban areas are five to six times higher than for young men. They also have little knowledge of how to prevent HIV – in African countries with generalized epidemics up to 80 per cent of women aged between 15 and 24 had insufficient knowledge to protect themselves. Nor can they protect themselves from rape and deliberate infection.

Mozambique's Prime Minister, Pascoal Mocumbi, reported in 2001 that the overall rate of infection among girls and young women in his country was twice that of boys their age: 'Not because the girls are promiscuous, but because nearly three out of five are married by age 18, 40 per cent of them to much older, sexually experienced men, who may expose their wives to HIV/AIDS. Abstinence is not an option for these child brides. Those who try to discuss condom use commonly face violence or rejection.'[19]

Responses that involve and treat young people – both men and women – and also deal with their relationships seem to be the best way of preventing HIV. As a result of specific campaigns, HIV prevalence among pregnant teenage girls in South Africa shrank by a quarter between 1998 and 2001. This, along with the drop in syphilis rates among pregnant women attending antenatal clinics – down to 2.8 per cent in 2001 from 11.2 per cent four years earlier – suggests that awareness campaigns and prevention programs are bearing fruit. In Addis Ababa, Ethiopia, HIV prevalence levels for women aged between 15 and 24 declined by more than a third between 1995 and 2001 as a result of targeted campaigns, although similar trends were not evident in outlying areas of the city. In Uganda the trend for young people is also downwards. Condom use by single women aged between 15 and 24 almost doubled between 1995 and 2001 and more women in that age group delayed sexual intercourse or abstained entirely.

However, abstinence is not the answer – even though a third of the latest $15 billion American funding for HIV/AIDS in Africa is now supposed to be conditional on abstinence programs. Adrienne Germain, president of the International Women's Health Coalition – a nonprofit group based in New York – believes that this stipulation could set back any progress that has been made in controlling the epidemic: 'There is no evidence that abstinence alone does the job. Most African women who have AIDS are monogamous and married. Their only risk factor is the behavior of their husbands.'[20]

It is now recognized that men's behavior drives the epidemic. Prevention programs are beginning to recognize that they need to target young men in particular, to provide them with information, to work on their self-respect as well as respect for young women, and to understand the pressures that they face, particularly where there are few job prospects and little to do.

'Around here there is only football, drink and sex. When it is dark there is only drink and sex. And when the drink runs out, there is sex,' said a young man from a rural area in Côte d'Ivoire.[21]

Peter Piot, UNAIDS Executive Director, noted on World Aids Day 2002: 'We need to remind ourselves of ways in which stigma and inequality push women to the end of the treatment queue, exacerbate HIV risks, sustain sexual violence and deprive girls of schooling. Yet we also need to remember that women's organizing in care, support and community education has been one key to success against the epidemic.'[22]

Women are the main carers of the old, the young and the sick. They also form the majority in the main caring professions. As such they make a major – and often unrecognized – contribution to the economy. In Britain about 15 per cent of women of working age are caring full-time for someone who is old, sick or disabled.

Occupational health

There are many steps between birth and death, and this chapter has looked at only a few health issues on that journey that relate particularly to women. Occupational health is another important area; many women's jobs still tend to be very different from men's jobs and the health risks also vary. This sexual division of labor affects women's health in six main ways:[23]

1. Women's jobs have specific characteristics (repetition, monotony, static effort) which may lead over time to changes in mental and physical health.
2. Spaces, equipment and schedules that are designed for men may not be suitable for women.
3. Occupational segregation may result in health risks for women and men by increasing monotony and repetition.
4. Gender-based job assignment may be vaunted as protecting the health of women and men and thus distract from more effective occupational-health promotion practices.
5. Discrimination against women is stressful of itself and may affect women's mental health.
6. Part-time workers (mainly women) are often excluded from adequate sickness benefits, maternity pay, holiday pay and the like.

Mental health

More women than men suffer from mental-health problems. Depression occurs two-to-three times more frequently in women than in men. The disparity in rates between men and women tends to be even more pronounced in the developing world.[24] In addition, women living in poor social and environmental circumstances with low levels of education and income, as well as difficult family and marital relationships, are much more likely than other women to suffer from mental disorders. Up to 20 per cent of those attending primary healthcare in developing countries suffer from anxiety and/or depressive disorders. In most centers these patients are not recognized and therefore not treated.

Disease and death

The things that women die of are changing. Because illness related to child bearing is such a serious problem in the South, it makes up three out of the ten leading causes of disease for women between the age of 15 and 44 worldwide.

Tuberculosis (TB) has become the single biggest infectious killer of women in the world.

'Wives, mothers and wage earners are being cut down in their prime and the world isn't noticing,' says Dr Paul Dolin of the World Health Organization's Global Tuberculosis Program. 'Yet the ripple effect on families, communities and economies will be felt long after a woman has died.'

In the US young women are developing 50 per cent more cancers than their grandmothers did. There has been a big increase in the number of deaths from breast cancer. Thirty years ago one in twenty women died of the disease; today the figure is one in eight. Deaths from breast cancer are related to access to medical care; in the US, for example, white women are more likely to get breast cancer, but black women are more likely to die from it.[25]

1 www.who.int/reproductive-health **2** www.who.int **3** http://www.who.int/mediacentre/releases/2003/pr77/en/ **4** Joni Seager, *The Atlas of Women: an economic, social and political survey*, The Women's Press, third edition, 2003. **5** http://www.unfpa.org/news/news.cfm?ID=154 &Language=1 **6** Judy Mirsky, *Birth rights: new approaches to safe motherhood*, Panos Institute, 2001. **7** Joni Seager, *The Atlas of Women: an economic, social and political survey*, The Women's Press, third edition, 2003. **8** http://www.unfpa.org/rh/planning.htm **9** www.mountainvoices.org **10** *Attacking Poverty*, World Development Report 2000/2001. **11** United Nations Department of Public Information DPI/1772/HR, February 1996. **12** www.who.int/reproductive-health **13** WHO maternal health and safe motherhood programme, (unpublished estimates). **14** http://www.unfpa.org/swp/1999/newsfeature3.htm **15** Suzanne Goldenberg, 'When does life really begin?', *The Guardian*, 6 June 2003. **16** DAWN, www.dawn.org **17** 'Current Practices and Controversies in Assisted Reproduction', www.who.int/reproductive-health **18** Policy paper on HIV/AIDS, Save the Children Fund [unpublished 2000]. **19** www.unaids.org/worldaidsday/2002/press/update/epiupdate2002/en.doc **20** http://www.wand.org/index.html **21** Thomas Scalway, *Young men and HIV: culture, poverty and sexual risk*, Panos Institute/UNAIDS, 2001. **22** www.unaids.org/worldaidsday/2002/press/update/epiupdate2002/en.doc **23** http://www.who.int/oeh/OCHweb/OCHweb/OSHpages/OSHDocuments/Women/ **24** World Bank, 1993 **25** Joni Seager, *The Atlas of Women: an economic, social and political survey*, The Women's Press, third edition, 2003.

3 Poverty, development and work

Women play a crucial role in development, but they have largely been ignored by attempts at poverty reduction. While globalization has brought about an explosion in the jobs market, the benefits for women have been mixed.

'Study after study has shown that there is no effective development strategy in which women do not play a central role. When women are fully involved, the benefits can be seen immediately; families are healthier and better fed; their income, savings and reinvestment go up. And what is true of families is also true of communities, and, in the long run, of whole countries.'

UN Secretary-General Kofi Annan[1]

Giving credit to microcredit

Ten million women have benefited from systems of small loans, also known as 'microcredit'.

- In 1997 the US granted more than 10,000 loans, totaling $67 billion, to women business owners worldwide
- In Belize the Small Farmers and Business Bank provided 29 per cent of its funds to women.
- Japan gave interest-free loans to 27,000 rural women.
- Since 1994, 96 per cent of Palestinian women in agricultural projects have benefited from loan programs.
- In Trinidad and Tobago the Small Business Development Company has distributed 65 per cent of its loans to women.
- In Sudan the United Nations Population Fund (UNFPA) has provided seed money for the establishment of commercial enterprises to raise the standard of living of low-income women.
- In Vietnam a project supported by the United Nations Children's Fund (UNICEF) has reached more than 60,000 poor women in 198 communes of 28 provinces, providing them with small loans and basic knowledge about income-generation activities. ■

United Nations Development Program's *Poverty Report* 1998.

IN THE LAST decade women have participated in development processes on a wider scale than ever before, even if only at small-scale level. For example, they have been the main actors in micro-credit schemes all over the world; they run their own businesses; they are involved at local-council level in many different countries.

The latest tools in the international development kit-box, the Poverty Reduction Strategy Papers (PRSPs), which are designed to benefit the poor through wide consultation with civil society, have largely ignored women. A recent study of four countries' PRSPs noted that: 'Women's voices have hardly been sought and have definitely not been heard. Women citizens are hardly consulted at all and gender advocates within national CSOs [Civil Society Organizations] are not heeded.'[2]

In addition, the very countries which are supposed to be benefiting from PRSPs suffered from the worldwide recession after 11 September 2001.

From WID to GAD: Confusions

From the 1970s to the 1990s development practice shifted from a focus on Women in Development (WID) to one on Gender and Development (GAD). While the terms 'woman' or 'man' refer to biological sex differences, 'gender' refers to masculine and feminine attributes that are shaped by society.

By moving from WID to GAD the focus shifted from women as a sex to the complex network of social, political and economic relationships between men and women. That means things like gender budgets and gender mainstreaming. The former puts resources behind initiatives on women, the latter views all aspects of development through a gender lens.

In theory the move towards gender analysis was positive. In practice the use of the word 'gender' in this context has often led to confusion and may have meant a lack of focus on women's rights in development.

For a more detailed discussion see 'Rethinking gender and development practice for the twenty-first century' by Judy El-Bushra, in *Gender in the 21st Century*, Oxfam 2002.

'We have seen the human toll the recent attacks wrought in the US, with citizens from some 80 nations perishing in New York, Washington and Pennsylvania,' said World Bank President James D Wolfensohn. 'But there is another human toll that is largely unseen and one that will be felt in all parts of the developing world, especially Africa. We estimate that tens of thousands more children will die worldwide and some ten million more people are likely to be living below the poverty line of $1 a day because of the terrorist attacks. This is simply from loss of income. Many, many more people will be thrown into poverty if development strategies are disrupted.'[3]

This exacerbated an already existing trend: in most countries the gap between rich and poor had been growing, and women made up a large proportion of the poor. The numbers of rural women living in poverty had doubled in twenty years.

The feminization of poverty

- The gap between women and men caught in the cycle of poverty has continued to widen in the past decade, a phenomenon commonly referred to as 'the feminization of poverty'.
- Seventy per cent of the 1.5 billion people living on $1 a day or less are women.
- Worldwide, women earn on average only slightly over 50 per cent of male earnings.
- Women living in poverty are often denied access to critical resources such as credit, land and inheritance. Their labor goes unrewarded and unrecognized. Their healthcare and nutritional needs are not given priority, they lack sufficient access to education and support services, and their participation in decision-making at home and in the community is minimal.
- Women constitute up to 90 per cent of all those working in Export Processing Zones (see below).
- Women lack access to the resources and services they need to change their situation. ■

The Feminization of Poverty, Factsheet No 1, United Nations.

Paid work

Much of women's work remains unrecognized, uncounted and unpaid; in the home, in agriculture, in food production and in childcare. Globalization has brought one main benefit to many women: more paid work. Since 1980 the growth in the labor force of women has been substantially higher than that of men in every region of the world except Africa (where the two labor forces have grown at the same rate). In Latin America the growth rate for women has been more than three times as great as that of men, at an annual average of over four per cent, while in the European Union 80 per cent of all labor-force growth is attributed to women's increasing participation.[4]

Professor Saud Choudhury of Canada's Trent University notes: 'The economic independence that these jobs provide has for the first time given Third World women the ability to contribute to their families financially; the opportunity to delay marriages and child-bearing; even the means to end oppressive marital relationships.'[5]

But while more women may be working, they are still paid less than men. In the US in 2000, on average, women earned 73 per cent of men's wages. Black and minority women fared even worse: African American women earned 63 cents and Latinas 56 cents to every dollar earned by males.[6] And women are often assigned to the worst-paid, shortest-contract, most monotonous jobs. In the 1990s the numbers of women part-timers increased in most industrialized countries. By the end of the decade in Japan and the US almost 70 per cent of all part-time workers were women. But 'where part-time work has been rising for women, it appears to be increasingly involuntary', says the International Labor Organization.[7]

In addition, there has been an increase in 'permanent temporary employment' where workers exist on a series of short-term contracts. Such employment is directed mainly at women and other discriminated-against groups. But their incorporation into global markets in this way has given them little security, few benefits, and no negotiating power. Such jobs are also vulnerable to external economic crises – it is estimated that during the collapse of the south and east Asian economies in 1998, 10,000 workers, most of them women, were laid off every day in South Korea.[8]

'This was inevitable,' comments the UN's Economic and Social Commission for Asia and the Pacific, 'given that women were originally preferred as workers largely because of the greater ease of dismissal.'

Victoria Tauli-Corpuz, director of the Tebtebba Foundation in the Philippines, says: 'Although globalization resulted in some women gaining employment in the manufacturing sector, the majority of Asian women are still found in the informal economy, rural farming communities, and in subsistence economic activities. The shifts in production patterns due to globalization… have led to the dislocation of women from their traditional sources of livelihood.'[9]

Transition countries

The World Bank's 2002 report *Gender in Transition* highlighted differences between men and women in the 27 'transition' countries (from the former Soviet bloc) in Europe and Central Asia. Pierella Paci, lead author of the report, says: 'Policy making in the region has often neglected the differential effects of transition on the welfare of men and women, thus increasing gender inequality and hampering socio-economic progress.'

For example, in Tajikistan the average working woman earns just over half the income of the average man. Girls are more malnourished than boys. Half as many girls as boys are enrolled in higher education. Nearly half of pregnant women do not receive any form of prenatal care, resulting in very high infant-mortality rates.

Kazakhstan has a higher level of income ($1,506 per capita in 2001) than its neighbors, but it has similarly disappointing reproductive health indicators. Women receive less than 70 per cent of men's wages despite often being more qualified.

A 2003 Human Rights Watch study in the Ukraine noted that: 'Women's post-Soviet experience in the labor force... reveals many worrying trends. According to local experts, the transition to a market economy has brought women "under-representation in decision-making positions, high rates of unemployment, and a re-emergence of traditional stereotypes concerning gender roles". During the Soviet period, over 90 per cent of women were employed or engaged in study, and women's share in the labor force exceeded men's in the 1970s and 1980s. But women's employment rate has been declining steadily from

Women in China

Capitalism has benefited an élite group of educated, urban women who are enjoying unprecedented opportunities – from heading to America for MBAs, to launching their own companies. But, in general, women are losing out. As discrimination against them increases, they are the first to be laid off from once-ironclad state jobs. They are the first to be deprived of local-government seats now that Beijing no longer enforces long-held gender quotas. They are the first to drop out of school as academic fees climb ever higher. And they have regressed financially, too: in the 1980s, women made 80 cents for every dollar that men earned; now, women make only 65 cents, as private enterprises are free to pay as they please. At the extremes, old bad habits from China's imperial past are also resurging: prostitution, concubinage, wife buying, female infanticide. One symptom of the intensifying pressure is that nearly 300,000 women in China committed suicide in 2000, making it the only country in the world where relatively more females than males take their own lives. 'China is progressing in so many ways,' says Deng Li, deputy director of the government-run All-China Women's Federation. 'But for many women, their lives are going backward, because the rules to protect them are no longer being followed.' ∎

http://www.time.com/time/asia/covers/501030728/story.html

1995 to 2000, reaching 52 per cent in 2000, far below the rate of 61 per cent among men.'[10]

Women in Export Processing Zones

Ninety per cent of the 27 million people working in export processing zones (EPZs) are women. EPZs have particular economic advantages which attract foreign investment. They produce textiles, sporting goods, electronics and footwear, often for Northern

---

The inside story:
conditions in Kenya's EPZs

Lucy Wairimu, 38, makes children's garments for export. Working eight hours a day she gets only $52 a month.

Wairimu's typical day begins at dawn when she prepares her four children for school, after which she walks the five kilometers to catch the 6.30 am factory truck to her place of work on the Mombasa road, some 10 kilometers away on the outskirts of the Kenyan capital of Nairobi.

Work begins at 7.00 am and she has only two short breaks before she clocks off. 'We are only allowed out of the premises after finishing our daily quota of at least four garments,' she says. Each garment fetches as much as 2,000 shillings ($33) in the market.

Wairimu's employer is one of the 24 enterprises running the export-processing zones (EPZs) sector, which have been hailed by the government of Kenya as a quick means of achieving economic growth. The EPZs, which employ some 9,000 people, are spread around the country, with three of them operating as industrial villages in Nairobi.

According to the Export Processing Zones Authority, the enterprises 'have done Kenya a lot of good'. In 1990 EPZs earned 900 million shillings ($15 million) in export revenue. By 1998 revenue had risen to 2.5 billion shillings ($42 million).

Human-rights groups, however, say the EPZs have not improved the lives of the 60 per cent of Kenya's population who live below the poverty line. Instead, they say, employees hired as cheap labor are subjected to poor working conditions while the firms make huge profits.

'When you look at the workers' input, you realize how much exploitation goes on in the factories,' says Lillian Adhiambo, a journalist in Nairobi. ∎

Jane Kariuki, Panos Features, April 1999.

markets. Pay levels for workers are often higher than outside the zone, but workers have long hours, limited job security and few opportunities for training or advancement. In many EPZs – for example, in Bangladesh, Pakistan and Zimbabwe – trade unions are banned. The advantages for women are questionable.

Vivian Stromberg, Executive Director of Madre, a US organization working with some of the world's poorest women, said: 'In our experience with recently opened markets, women are virtual prisoners in many factories, subject to physical violence including sexual

The Free Trade Area of the Americas

A Free Trade Area of the Americas (FTAA) is being proposed that would extend NAFTA (the North American Free Trade Area, comprising the US, Canada and Mexico) to South America and create the world's largest free-trade zone by 2005. It would affect 650 million people and $9 trillion in capital. Regulations on foreign investment would be minimal. Governments would have to treat foreign investors in the same way as domestic businesses. National environmental and worker-protection laws would be bypassed. Some of the potential effects on women and poor people have already been seen under NAFTA in Mexico:

- A rapid increase in the incorporation of women in workplaces where salaries are low and social benefits almost non-existent, such as the pharmaceutical and textile industries, and as domestic workers.
- Poor women increasingly being obliged to do a 'triple working day' – paid work, unpaid work in the household, and community management.
- Cuts in health and education programs and food subsidies; women have to spend more time substituting for services previously provided by the state.
- The frequent closure of factories and reductions in the workforce have a direct effect on women and also lead to increased levels of violence against women and children, impacting on the physical and mental health of poor families. ■

'Women's legal knowledge: a case study of Mexican urban dwellers', Luisa Maria Rivera Izabal, in *Women and Rights*, edited by Caroline Sweetman, Oxfam 1998.

assault, strip searches, attacks on union organizers, and forced consumption of amphetamines to increase output. Women work longer hours than their male counterparts, are paid half the wages, and suffer from serious work-related health problems, including lung damage, memory loss and numbness from exposure to toxic materials.'[11]

Migration and trafficking in women

The movement of people across borders brought about by globalization has meant that women can move around more independently than ever before. Migration can provide women with new opportunities, financial independence and status in their home country. Almost 50 per cent of the world's 175 million migrants are women. In some regions this number is even higher.[12] Women migrants often send remittances home. In their host countries they have many skills to bring but are still often considered second-class citizens.

In Asia, women are now the majority of expatriates working abroad. This has been a big change over the last 20 years, when migrants were mainly men. In Sri Lanka, between 1986 and 1999, female migrant workers increased from 33 per cent to 65 per cent of the total migrant workforce. In 1999 remittances from Sri Lankan female migrant workers accounted for 50 per cent of the country's trade balance and 45 per cent of gross foreign loans and grants.

In the Philippines in 2000 women accounted for 70 per cent of migrant workers abroad. Most traveled alone and were the main providers for their families back home. Filipina women migrants contributed $6.2 billion in total remittances for 2001.[13]

But, says the International Organization for Migration (IOM), 'women migrants are more exposed to forced labor, sexual exploitation and violence than men and are also more likely to accept precarious working conditions and lower wages'.

Globalization has contributed to a worldwide growth in the numbers of women and girls being trafficked for forced sexual services. Trafficking has become one of the fastest-growing criminal activities in the global economy, with between 700,000 and two million women involved every year, a large proportion

Sexual slavery in Montenegro

Montenegro and the Balkans generally are known to be both transit countries as well as destinations used by traffickers of women and girls. Most of the victims come from Eastern Europe – in the Balkans it is estimated that some 60 per cent of trafficked women and girls come from Moldova, one of Europe's poorest countries. Many victims are lured by promises of work in Western Europe as waitresses or similar but are forced into sexual slavery. Many are broken mentally and physically by rape and extreme brutality.

Recently a high-profile trial collapsed after the Prosecutor's Office in Podgorica, the capital of Montenegro, halted criminal proceedings against the Deputy State Prosecutor and three other men for involvement in sex slavery.

The main witness, a 28-year-old mother of two from Moldova, suffered horrendous sexual abuse for over three years, resulting in severe injuries including seven broken bones, internal injuries so that she cannot sit down without pain, scars from handcuffs, cigarette burns on her genitals, and bruises in her mouth. She alleged that Montenegrin politicians, judges, police and civil servants had tortured and raped her and other East European women who, like her, had been trafficked and held as sex slaves.

'The halt in criminal proceedings has led to allegations of a cover-up by the Montenegrin authorities,' say Amnesty International. 'The trafficking of women and girls as sex slaves is a major concern and the collapse of this case, despite apparent detailed evidence and testimony, can only cast doubt on the Montenegrin authorities' commitment to fight this inhuman trade. Her story is consistent with many other horrifying tales of women and girls forced into sexual slavery. She had come to Serbia from Moldova looking for work. After handing over her passport she became a slave, sold on to different "owners" as if she were an animal, routinely beaten, drugged, burned and raped.'

She alleges that whenever she tried to escape she was handed back to her 'owners' by the police until she finally managed to reach the Women's Safe House in Podgorica in November 2002. ■

Amnesty International news release, 5 June 2003.

of whom are sold many times over. The UN estimates that four million people were trafficked in 1998 and the industry is worth five to seven billion dollars a year.[14]

The IOM's Deputy Director General, Ndioro Ndiaye, noted: 'As long as there is a demand and market for trafficking in persons, the human-rights abuses it entails will continue. Unsuccessful economic transition, bad governance, corruption and gender-based discrimination caused by deep-rooted patriarchal structures also aggravate the problem of trafficking in women.'[15]

Economic crises and disparities between countries fuel supply, while economic liberalization has led to a demand for cheap labor. Where economic growth has meant an expanding middle class – as in Indonesia, Malaysia and the Philippines – men have more money to buy sexual services. In other countries, widespread poverty has meant that women are lured by the promise of a good job in another country – though few know what they face when they arrive. Traffickers exploit women's desire to make a better life for themselves with promises of jobs as waitresses, dancers, models, maids and nannies. Once they arrive, their passports are taken away and they are forced to work as prostitutes. And even if they manage to escape, their families will often not have them back as they have been 'dishonored'.

1 Speech on International Women's Day, 8 March 2003. **2** Ann Whitehead, *Failing women, sustaining poverty: Gender in Poverty Reduction Strategy Papers*, report for the UK Gender and Development Network, May 2003. **3** 'Poverty to Rise in Wake of Terrorist Attacks in US: Millions More People Condemned to Poverty in 2002.' World Bank, 10 January 2002. **4** *Globalization and employment: new opportunities, real threats*, Panos briefing 33, May 1999. **5** Saud Choudhury, 'Women Workers in the Global Factory: Impact of Gender Power Asymmetries', in *The Political Economy of Globalization,* quoted in Panos briefing 33 above. **6** www.wilpf.org **7** *Key Indicators of the Labour Market 2001-2002*, ILO, Geneva, 2002. **8** *Globalisation and employment: new opportunities, real threats*, Panos briefing 33, May 1999. **9** Victoria Tauli-Corpuz, 'Asia-Pacific women grapple with financial crisis and globalization', in *Third World Resurgence*, no 94, June 1998. **10** http://www.hrw.org/reports/2003/ukraine0803 **11** www.madre.org/art_manyfaces.html **12** *World Migration report 2003*, IOM. **13** http://www.iom.int/en/news/pr858_en.shtml **14** Coalition against Trafficking in Women, 2001. **15** http://www.iom.int/en/news/pr858_ en.shtml

4 Shopping and talking: woman as global consumer

Globalization has changed the face of the world, making us all into global consumers and giving us access to instant information. This has deeply affected women's lives.

'Despite new initiatives and commitments, the sad reality is that the situation of the world's women is progressively deteriorating due to globalization.'
Ramachandra Reddy, India, at the Social, Humanitarian and Cultural Committee of the UN General Assembly, October 2000.[1]

WHEN THE PEOPLE of the future look back on this century and the last, globalization is likely to be seen as its defining feature. People flying around the world, instant communication between continents, the spread of free trade and the rise of a global consumer culture.

Globalization has been defined as: 'The process in which economic, financial, technical and cultural transactions between different countries and communities around the world are increasingly interconnected and embody common elements of experience, practice and understanding.'[2]

The global consumer

For those who have money, globalization has led to a world in which choice is king and the consumer is the champion. In a world where, as ex-British Prime Minister Margaret Thatcher once famously said: 'There is no such thing as society', everyone has become an individual, a 'consumer', someone to be marketed at. An increasingly consumerist culture sees shopping, not politics or rights, as the solution to our woes – more people vote on the television show

'Big Brother' than vote in elections. And the ways that women have been marketed at, and used for marketing, have changed considerably in the last decade.

Advertisements reinforce the view of the 'ideal' woman's body. Few women's bodies conform to this ideal, and increasing numbers are opting for cosmetic surgery in order to pursue the illusion of youth and beauty.

Women and advertising

Each person in the US sees around 1,500 advertisements every day. The advertising industry is worth $320 billion a year.

In the 1980s women defaced advertising posters that were considered to be sexist. Today, it seems, women's bodies can once again be used to sell cars or perfume. True, men are sometimes portrayed as fathers as well as lovers or powerful businessmen, but women's bodies have become objects once more. But now, no-one complains. In a recent internet poll, respondents were asked to vote on the question: Has the portrayal of women in advertising improved over the last 10 years? Seven per cent said that advertisers were more respectful of women, 23 per cent said some improvement had been made and an overwhelming 70 per cent said 'no, the majority of ads portray women in stereotypical roles.' ∎

http://www.aef.com/poll-fu.asp?poll=1951

Cosmetic surgery is being used by younger and younger women.

'A girl ought to have the right to decide whether she wants breast implants if she is an otherwise normal 16-year-old with little breast development,' says Paul Weiss, a member of the American Society of Plastic Surgeons.

'It is totally common for people to have their eyes done, their chins implanted, their ears pinned back,' says Mara, aged 17, from New York City Women's College. 'Plastic surgery is more and more accepted, and people do it either in fifth grade or after high school, before college.'[3]

In one year in the US, the number of cosmetic surgical interventions on girls aged under 18 jumped by 21.8 per cent, from 65, 231 to 79,051.[4] Surgery can cost thousands of dollars. Many girls work and go into debt in order to pay for the operation they think will change their lives.

Top five surgical procedures in the US

Cosmetic surgery has increased more than five-fold in ten years. Women now have nearly a million operations in order to conform to the 'ideal' face or body. And this includes increasing numbers of teenagers.

	1992	2002
Breast augmentation	32,607	236,888
Liposuction	47,212	282,876
Nose reshaping	50,175	354,327
Eyelid surgery	59,461	230,672
Facelift	40,077	117,831
Total	229,532	1,222.594

This desire to look 'perfect' also affects young women's eating habits. More than half of teenage girls are, or think they should be, on a diet. In a 1998 survey by Exeter University in Britain, 57.5 per cent of 37,500 young women aged between 12 and 15 listed 'appearance' as the biggest concern in their lives.

In the US, anorexia – defined as 'the relentless pursuit of thinness' – affects one out of every hundred young women. Some have literally starved themselves to death. Bulimia, where women binge eat and then make themselves sick, affects four in every hundred. Ninety per cent of people with these disorders are female. Most are in their teens and twenties.

It is this age group that is at the sharp end of aggressive marketing campaigns.

Shopping for America

For a month after 11 September 2001... we thought we would never go back to being interested in seeing Sisqo on the cover of *Teen People*, or in who the star of *7th Heaven* is. We thought we would never again care how much Britney got to sell burgers for McDonald's, or whether she had lost her virginity to Justin Timberlake and whether that possibility improved the ratings of her HBO concert. We now lived in another era, a precinct of elevation and suffering, and all the pap of teens appeared obsolete.

An article in *Salon* claimed that the 'bright side to the obscene events' of September 11 is that Britney Spears and the Backstreet Boys, Total Request Live and Limp Bizkit, Survivor, Sony Playstation and N Sync will never be enough. 'Everything changed on September 11,' the writer asserted, 'bringing about the sudden realization for many that their current opiates were nothing but placebos.' Others predicted the end of teen-propelled reality television, writing the genre into the past tense. 'On September 11 Americans got a dose of true reality.' An article in the *Hartford Courant* read: 'How can people watch a show called "Survivor" when so many people are simply trying to survive?'

Within a month, though, the mourning was transformed in to patriotism. Mall-going was prescribed as the contemporary version of planting the victory garden. Go to the mall, teenagers were told, along with the rest of us. Delia's sold many T-shirts emblazoned with the Manhattan skyline and American flags. We were asked to shell out cash for brand-name goods. The kids got the message: 'It's patriotic to shop.' ■

Alissa Quart, *Branded: the buying and selling of teenagers*,
Arrow, 2003.

Women and technology

New technologies are an inextricable part of globalization and are in the business of transforming people's lives. They also have gender distinctions and the potential to make women's lives better – or worse.

For example, ever since Dolly the sheep was cloned in 1997, there has been considerable debate – and some unusual alliances – between those in favor of cloning and those against. Because women bear children, women's organizations have been in the forefront of these discussions.

Cloning involves taking an egg from a female and using it to create another being identical in its DNA to the first. Gene transplantation techniques involve the selection of certain genes for a fetus.

For financial reasons, cloning experiments are done within the corporate sector, by researchers who work either for biotechnology companies or in university laboratories with significant financial stakes in the success of commercial enterprises.

Women's groups say that such technologies would: 'Move decisions about reproduction further away from women, not only toward doctors and technicians but also toward marketers proffering the "enhancements" developed by biotech companies.' They say that women may find themselves losing more and more control over childbearing, under pressure to do all they can to produce the 'perfect baby'.[5]

Disability-rights activists note that prenatal screening already makes it possible for women to abort babies not considered 'perfect' or to choose male over female babies. These developments would put women in the position of 'eugenic gatekeepers', able to choose not only whether to have a certain baby but, eventually, whether that baby would have blue eyes or brown, be short or tall, good-looking or intelligent. Even if this were desirable, what of the many parents who could not afford to have their children genetically enhanced in this way?

At present, cloning is still a dangerous business. Fundamental questions remain, not least: in a market economy, who would decide what was on offer to whom? [6]

Information technology

Women still lag behind men in most countries in their use of information technology. While they make up 42 per cent of all internet users globally, this ranges from almost nothing in some countries to over 50 per cent in Canada and the US.[7] Seventy-nine per cent of internet users are in the rich world. There are some fundamental problems to increasing women's access – in Africa, for example, rural women are predominantly illiterate. One study in Guinea-Bissau showed that 74 per cent of women were illiterate.[8] In addition, in least developed countries, only one person in 200 even has access to a telephone and many areas may not even have electricity.

Why women don't use communications technology

In a survey by the International Telecommunications Union, women were asked to rank the most important obstacles to using information communications technologies (ICTs). These ranged from 'awareness of ICTs' and the ability to read, to problems with access to communication and lack of time.

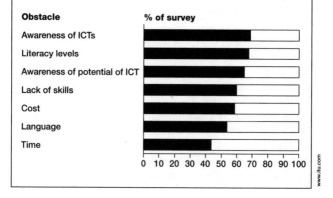

Obstacle	% of survey
Awareness of ICTs	
Literacy levels	
Awareness of potential of ICT	
Lack of skills	
Cost	
Language	
Time	

0 10 20 30 40 50 60 70 80 90 100

www.itu.com

However, the same survey showed that 92 per cent of women believed access to the internet to be crucial to women's development. 'Unless African women can participate fully in cyberspace, they will face a new form of exclusion from society,' says Marie-Helene Mottin-Sylla of the Synergy, Gender and Development

Program of ENDA Tiers Monde in Senegal.[9] Ease of communication has also meant many internet-based jobs are among those moving to the South. This brings work to women in Bangalore or Barbados, but it also begs many questions.

The new factory

'A hundred Barbadian women sit at rows of computer terminals. They enter 300,000 ticket reservations flowing from 2,000 daily flights of just a single US airline. In the same building one floor above them other women enter data from American medical insurance claims. Their average hourly wage is only $2.50 compared with the same company's $9.50 hourly wage for its US-based employees.

If you make a plane reservation nowadays more than likely it will be processed by these women sitting at their work stations in Barbados, or their sisters in Jamaica, St Kitts-Nevis, Haiti, India, Singapore, China or Ireland.' ∎

'Silicon tricks and the two dollar woman', Cynthia Enloe, *New Internationalist*, no 227, January 1992.

What is not in doubt is that connection brings many benefits for women. Fadia Faqir, the co-ordinator for the Center of Middle Eastern Women Studies at Durham University in England says: 'Women in Jordan have access to the internet and 45 satellite channels, and because of that exposure, have aspirations that they can change their lives. If you can look in your neighbor's garden and you see an alternative, you start thinking of alternatives for yourself.'

The internet also makes global campaigning possible – for example, the Asia Monitor Research Centre joined forces with the London-based World Development Movement, the British Trades Union Congress and other groups across Europe to achieve better conditions for workers in Asia's toy-producing factories.

The 2003 World Summit on the Information Society aimed to examine the information revolution and its impact on people's lives. But its declaration of principles has been criticized by women's groups because it 'does not explicitly confront the fact that fundamental political, social and economic inequalities shape our world', and does not 'adequately recognize the centrality of gender inequality to broader social inequality'.[10]

Net statistics

- In the US the number of women using the internet jumped from 38 per cent in 1996 to 51 per cent in 2000. Nonetheless, the percentage of women in the overall information-technology (IT) workforce fell from 41 per cent to 34.9 per cent between 1996 and 2002.
- In Thailand the share of female internet users jumped from 35 per cent in 1999 to 49 per cent in 2000.
- In Brazil women account for 47 per cent of internet users.
- From April 2001 to April 2002, the percentage of female internet users who access the web at home grew in every key market in Asia except Australia. ■

Information Technology Association of America; www.nua.com

New authority
One of the positive aspects of globalization has been the thousands of women's organizations that have emerged over the last 20 years campaigning on a wide range of different development issues, from HIV/AIDS to the environment, political representation to poverty. This has given many women a new authority with which to counter some of the negative effects of the globalization process.

'We are outraged at the destruction and right-wing opportunism that have gripped the world since September 11. But our work with other women whose lives, families and communities are on the front lines of the world's most entrenched conflicts gives us tremendous strength,' says the women's organization Madre.[11]

Shopping and talking

1 http://www.twnside.org.sg/title/height.htm 2 R Pearson, 'Moving the goalposts: gender and globalization in the twenty-first century' *Gender and Development* vol 8 (1) 2000. 3 Alissa Quart, *Branded: the buying and selling of teenagers*, Arrow, 2003. 4 Alissa Quart, *Branded: the buying and selling of teenagers*, Arrow, 2003. 5 Council for responsible genetics, article by Marcy Darnovsky http://www.gene-watch.org/genewatch/articles/14-4germlinewomen.html 6 See www.puaf.umd.edu/IPPP/Fall97Report/cloning.htm and http://www.gene-watch.org/genewatch/articles/14-4germlinewomen.html 7 www.itu.com 8 www.idrc.ca/acacia/outputs/womenicts.html#Introduction 9 *The Internet and Poverty, Real Help or Real Hype?* Panos, 1998. 10 The Association for Progressive Communication (APC) Women's Programme. 11 www.madre.org

5 Women and the environment: making the long march longer

Changes to the environment are gender specific. Women are rarely able to take part in decisions about their environment, whether the issue is the privatization of water, the ownership of land or the patenting of seeds. But they have done much to protect it, sometimes at great risk to themselves.

'Probably no other group is more affected by environmental destruction than poor village women. Every dawn brings with it the long march in search of fuel, fodder and water... As ecological conditions worsen, the long march becomes even longer and more tiresome. Caught between poverty and environmental destruction, poor rural women in India could well be reaching the limits of physical endurance.'

Centre for Science and Environment in India[1]

IS THERE A difference between women's and men's relationship to the environment? What does this have to do with women's rights?

At first glance the environment of the world, and sustainable ways to develop it, do not seem to be gender-specific. Climate change and global warming, deforestation, pollution, the depletion of global water resources, environmental degradation and disaster affect every human being on the planet, whatever their sex.

But, in fact, research shows that environmental issues can affect men and women very differently. This can be illustrated by women's relationship to water. While women often have clearly defined responsibilities, they rarely have control over water resources or access to decision-making about water. And yet, says Indian environmentalist Vandana Shiva: 'In the Third World women carry the water to get it home. They are the ones first to know water is polluted. They are the first to know the well has run dry. They are the first to know water is saline. They are the canary of the eco-crisis.'[2]

They are also often at the forefront of environmental battles.

Saved from the crocodiles

Lordes is afraid of crocodiles. In the dry season the water in the river where she lives dries out and she has to walk to the main river. Carrying her bucket, she tries to find a safe place to scoop up the water. But she knows that the river is full of crocodiles and piranhas. Each day the journey can take several hours, but once the bucket is full and balanced on her head she no longer cares about the journey home. She is safe.

Last year, for the first time, she didn't have to make the long journey to the crocodiles – thanks to a new project where she lives in the Mamiraua Sustainable Development Reserve, northeastern Brazil.

The majority of the 6,000 people in the villages where Lordes lives are small-scale farmers. But during the wet season, when the water can rise up to 12 metres, the fields are flooded for three months and crops cannot be grown. The floods bring rubbish and sewage waste. Her five children often become ill around this time. This makes life even harder as she has to look after them as well as cook and clean and work and find water.

Until last year the area had no electricity. But now, with the use of solar-energy pumps, Lordes' life has changed for the better. The water is pumped to a high reservoir and then distributed by gravity to households. Each now has a tap by the door and everyone has a period in the day when they can use the water.

Lordes was part of the group which decided where the pumps should go and is responsible for maintaining the pumps now that they are up and running. Many of her neighbors are also part of the group, as women make up at least a quarter of the membership. In addition, she has time to look after her family, work in the fields and even think about learning to read. And she is no longer afraid of the crocodiles. ■

Adapted from 'A case study in the Brazilian Amazon region: a gender approach to energy supply' by Adelia del Melo Branco, *ENERGIA News* vol 5 no 4, 2002.

No more plastic bags

Supriya Sahu is not an obvious fighter. But as District Collector in the Ooty region of Southern India she has taken on the business lobby in her effort to ban plastic bags from the area.

And she has won. A law has been enacted. Large signposts greet visitors entreating them to 'Enjoy your stay in the Nilgiris, but please do not use plastic'. Chellerams, one of the biggest stores, was fined 1,000 rupees for disregarding the ban.

All over the district the traditional Tamil manja pye – a colored cloth bag – has reappeared. Meat and fish are wrapped in leaves as they used to be 10 years ago. And school children frequently go on plastic-picking treks.

In this ecologically sensitive and tourism-prone region plastics had not only caused mountains of litter but suffocated animals, choked drainage and water-supply channels and polluted Ooty Lake.

Young, bright and determined, Supriya Sahu has begun the process of reversing the damage. ∎

www.hinduonnet.com/thehindu/2002/05/26/stories/
2002052600091200.htm

Privatizing the earth

Privatization, industrial logging, over-fishing, toxic dumping, mining… the effects of the free market and globalization on the environment and the threat that this poses to its sustainability have been well documented. The latest solution to the world's environmental problems, it seems, is not to cut down on our use of fossil fuels, or to find better ways of conserving water and less polluting chemicals for everyday use, but to privatize environmental resources.

The issue of privatization has particular problems for women. For example, in Ghana and elsewhere the privatization of water has led to an increase in waterborne diseases such as typhoid, cholera and guinea worm among the poor, who cannot afford to pay for clean water. A bucket of water costs up to a tenth of people's daily earnings in cities. And finding water for their families has become an even bigger burden for women. Says Hawa Amadu, who lives in one of Accra's slum areas: 'Sometimes I go without food so my grandchildren will have water... Soon we will have to drink air.'[3]

Privatization of land, however, can have positive effects if women are allowed to own and control it. Florence Nnali, a landless farm worker in Uganda who survives by collecting wild cassava for herself and her six children, says: 'Land in Uganda is wealth. You cannot have land and starve. If you have land you can plant crops on it, sell it and be buried on it.'[4]

But there is a hidden danger, says environmentalist Bina Agarwal. The buying of land by women can be 'used by pro-liberalization lobbies to open up indigenous systems of land tenure to market forces and foreign commercial interests'.[5]

Green beans

When Irene Kathambi's husband first sold her the idea of growing French beans in Marathi village, Meru, she thought she would have equal claim over the proceeds. 'I do most of the work on the farm such as digging, planting, weeding and picking. But my husband receives the payments and gives me what he pleases after we have sold the crop,' she says.

There are many women like Irene Kathambi, whose husbands have either compelled them to grow green beans on their plots, or retracted their right to these plots entirely. A study notes that 'export horticulture' has changed from being a predominantly female sphere to a mixed one, which has a knock-on effect on property control. It estimates that women carry out more than 70 per cent of the labor for French beans but receive only 30 per cent of the income. Under the traditional system of land rights in Kenya, women have the rights to cultivate land but not to own it – and access is usually given through a male relative.

Like Irene, most Meru women don't inherit or own land. Armed with only 'use rights' women cannot prevent men from encroaching on their plots. ∎

Francis Ayieko in *Food for All? Can hunger be halved?* John Madeley, Panos Institute, 2001.

Women's health

The environment has an effect on women's health as well as their income. Millions of women who are forced to cook on open fires, or to carry heavy containers long distances every day to collect water, may find that their health suffers as a result. Pollution and pesticide use also cause problems for women; there is a link between environmental pollution and cancers such as breast cancer. Endocrine-disrupting chemicals have been shown to breach the placenta, reach babies in the womb and infect breast milk, resulting in thyroid problems, delayed sexual development and sometimes lower IQ in children.[6]

The incidence of breast cancer also relates to environmental factors. 'Breast cancer activists are increasingly certain that environmental factors, including exposure to plastics-based estrogen-mimicking chemicals, are responsible for the near-epidemic rates of the disease,' says Joni Seager.

Other chemicals can cross national boundaries, and build up in the food chain. These are known as POPS – Persistent Organic Pollutants. Nine of the 12 most polluting and harming to health are pesticides, used extensively in agriculture. And 60 to 70 per cent of the world's farmers and agricultural workers are women – 80 per cent in some parts of Africa. The World Health Organization estimates that at least three million people are poisoned by pesticides every year and more than 200,000 die.[7]

In Malaysia, for example, many women work on the plantations and spray pesticides. They suffer from sore eyes, skin complaints, burnt fingernails and disrupted menstruation. Pregnant women have been known to lose their babies or give birth to deformed babies. Veena is one of the sprayers:

'I have been spraying pesticides for the past 20 years. I spray paraquat all the time.[8] It is so strong that the odor makes me sick most of the time. In the beginning I used to cry. Now my only main problem is nose bleed and chest pain. I also have bad stomach pain.'[9]

Climate change and disasters

Climate change and disasters also have a direct impact on poor women, who are responsible for family and community care, and as such are key to the survival of both. Environmental crises mean that they have to spend even more time finding food and shelter, and walking further to fetch water or cut firewood. 'Growing desertification caused by changed farming practices in fragile ecosystems also forces women to walk for miles in search of water,' says Madhukar Upadhya, research director of the Nepal Water Conservation Foundation. 'Women in Sindh in Pakistan walk up to 10 miles to fetch water and women with pitchers trudging up steep slopes is a common sight in the hills.'[10]

And yet neither the Kyoto Protocol nor the UN Framework Convention for Climate Change (UNFCCC) makes any mention of gender, and there has been very little research or discussion on the effects of climate change on women.

In 1998 Hurricane Mitch affected more than two million people in Honduras and Nicaragua alone. Damages were estimated at $5 billion. Small producers, street children and female-headed households were hardest hit. Women had to maintain their households, help organize the community and find work in the informal economy. They had more to do, and less to eat. After the disaster, men had generally tried to go back to their old jobs, but women found it more diffi-cult because of their many responsibilities. Cultural roles may make women more at risk than men during environmental disasters. In the 1991 floods in Bangladesh 71 women died for every 15 men. Most were drowned because they were not supposed to leave their homes and stayed there until it was too late. They were also less likely than men to be able to swim. [11]

Disasters aside, even a heavy rainy season or a drought can have a significant impact on the hours women have to put in just to keep themselves and their families alive.[12] 'The disproportionate share of the burden of poverty borne by women has a two-fold impact,' says Madhukar Upadhya. 'On the one hand, their workload for family survival increases and, on the other, their share in food and nutrition intake decreases further. In almost all countries of the region [South Asia] women do not have an adequate calorific intake in their diet and many pregnant women suffer from anemia.'[13] Indigenous women in particular, who have a close relationship with the land on which they live, are deeply affected by any changes to their environment:

'Our entire life depends on forests. We get firewood from forests, wood for house construction and also fodder for our cattle... We also get grass, leaves, precious herbs and minerals for our animals. In addition, forests give us tea leaves, humus, fertilizer,' says Lakupati, an 80-year-old tribal woman from Kinnaur, India.[14]

Patenting

Indigenous women have been heavily involved in opposing the patenting of products, plants and processes through what is known as the agreement on Trade Related Aspects of Intellectual Property Rights (TRIPS). This agreement, signed in 1993, extends international patenting rights to all members of the World Trade Organization and stipulates that all member countries must introduce a new and standardized level of patent protection. Diverse Women for Diversity, a women's organization, argues that the patenting of seeds and other natural resources such as the *neem* tree has an adverse effect on rural women: 'Intellectual property rights (IPRs)... will dispossess rural women of their power, control and knowledge. IPRs... aim to take seed out of peasant women's custody and medical plants out of the hands of women healers and make it the private property of transnational companies.'[15]

In effect, their argument is that the patenting of seeds not only threatens biodiversity by giving companies 'ownership' of seeds, but undermines women's roles as the guardians and custodians of plants, whether as farmers or as traditional healers. 'There are 7,500 species used as medicinal plants by the indigenous medical traditions of India. These traditions are kept alive by over 400,000 [practitioners], in addition to millions of housewives, birth attendants and herbal healers using village-based health traditions. Seventy per cent of healthcare needs in India are still based on traditional systems using medicinal plants. Eighty per cent of seeds used by farmers still come from farmers' seed supply. India is thus still a predominantly biodiversity-based economy and women's knowledge is very central to this economy.'[16]

Women fight back

And yet women have been mainly absent from most of the big decisions taken about the environment. At the sixth Conference of Parties to the UNFCCC meeting (known as CoP6) in the Hague in November 2000, women's issues were barely on the agenda, although Jan Pronk, the Chair(man), when interviewed afterwards, noted that: 'In developing countries women are often the primary providers and users of energy. Therefore, the participation of women and women's organizations is crucial.'

The fact that women's issues were not part of the debate was all the more surprising in that as many as 20 per cent of environment ministers at the conference were women and so were representatives from three main non-governmental organizations (NGOs): Friends of the Earth, Worldwide Fund for Nature and the Climate Action Network.[17] Some of the key NGO negotiators are women, who may even be interested in gender issues at an individual level and yet 'in the heat of the negotiations, they seem to get absorbed by the complex technical issues', says Gotelind Alber of the Climate Alliance.[18]

In other international fora, women are generally discussed only as an add-on, as Jyothi Parika of the West African NGO, ENDA Tiers-Monde, noted in her workshop – which was the only one on women – at CoP8 (on climate change) in New Delhi in October 2002. Many women at such conferences – including the World Summit on Social Development in Johannesburg in 2002 – call for capacity building and advocacy work to improve women's voices at these conferences.

Women are also absent from senior levels in businesses dealing with the environment – in the energy sector in Germany, for example, women make up six per cent of technical staff, four per cent of decision-makers and only one per cent of senior managers. 'Many countries in the South have a much better track record than in the North in encouraging women to follow technical studies,' notes Ulrike Roehr, a German civil engineer and founder of Frauen Umweltnetz (Women's Environmental Network).[19]

Defending the environment
But, increasingly, women are joining together to defend their environment and to present sustainable solutions. In the 1970s the women of the Chipko movement in northern India saved the forests in their area by attaching themselves to individual trees to stop them being cut down. Since then thousands of women's groups, from the grassroots to the international, have formed. Some are very specific, like Chipko or ENERGIA or AWLAE (African Women Leaders in Agriculture and the Environment). Others work on a range of issues – a few examples from many are Environment and Development Action in the Third World (ENDA-TM); Women's Environmental

Networks in various European countries; Diverse Women for Diversity; the Grassroots Organizations operating together in Sisterhood (GROOTS), and the Women's Environment and Development Network (WEDO).

At the 1992 UN Conference on Environment and Development women came up with their own comprehensive blueprint for change. Formulated by 1,500 women from 83 countries and covering a broad range of critical issues, the Women's Action Agenda 21 helped galvanize women worldwide to push for their priorities in international institutions, governments, the private sector and civil society. There are now 3,500 Local Agenda 21s in the world – though only six in the US.

In the lead-up to the 2002 UN World Summit on Sustainable Development (WSSD) in Johannesburg,

---

Profile: Wangari Maathai

Wangari Maathai was in trouble again. This time it was for protesting against the building of a $200 million skyscraper in Kenya's Uhuru (Freedom) Park, in downtown Nairobi. The ruling party planned to have its offices in the park, and Maathai has publicly complained: 'We can provide parks for rhino and elephants; why can't we provide open spaces for the people? Why are we creating environmental havoc in urban areas?'

The money would mostly be borrowed from foreign banks, said Maathai. 'We already have a debt crisis; we owe billions to foreign banks now. And the people are starving. They need food; they need medicine; they need education. They do not need a skyscraper to house the ruling party and a 24-hour TV station.'

As a result of her outspokenness, the President called her a 'mad woman' and a 'threat to the order and security of the country', and has called for the public and the police to 'stamp out trouble-makers'. Parliament called her a 'sentimental frustrated divorcee' and accused her of inciting people to rise against 'the government of men'.

But this was in 1998 – and the skyscraper has still not been built. Maathai is used to slander. She is also used to being beaten and imprisoned for her beliefs. As a leading member of Kenya's women's movement, a public critic of her government and a prominent figure in the global environmental lobby, she is often in trouble.

women around the world collaborated to update and revitalize the agenda for change. The new Women's Action Agenda for a Peaceful and Healthy Planet 2015 is a vision for the future and a document of principles that people worldwide can contribute to and use for their own advocacy globally, nationally and locally. It covers peace and human rights, globalization for sustainability, access and control of resources, environmental security and health and governance for sustainable development.

Hand in hand

Women's rights and environmental improvement go hand-in-hand: 'The sustainable use of natural resources can only be achieved in the long term if the approach includes the concept of women's autonomy. However, women's autonomy can only be

In 1964 she founded the National Council of Women in Kenya. In 1977 she started the Greenbelt Movement to counter the environmental consequences of deforestation and desertification and to educate people about development that is truly sustainable. Greenbelt started with a tree nursery in Maathai's garden; today over 20 million trees have been planted in Kenya and there are 5,000 tree nurseries. Projects in other countries have also modeled themselves on Greenbelt.

'The biggest impact,' says Maathai, 'has been the sense of hope and power in the lives of the ordinary women who comprise 90 per cent of the members. They can hardly read or write. Yet they often join the movement not from personal need; instead they need to help their family – they need to get money to pay their children's school fees or to buy their clothes or to build a house. And the women respond so quickly to a common cause that soon they see this as a way to help the community at large – and the nation. They want to make a contribution.'

She became Deputy Minister in the Ministry of Environment, Natural Resources and Wildlife in January 2003 under the new president Mwai Kibabi.

Imprisoned, battered but unbeaten, she continues to make her voice, and the voice of thousands of Kenyan women, heard to protect their environment – and ours. ∎

www.chatham.edu/rci/well/women11-20/maathai.html

strengthened if account is taken of elements relating to the use of natural resources,' says a paper from the Dutch Ministry of Foreign Affairs.[20]

But this can only happen when account is taken of both at the same time. An Action Aid study of girls in Nepal showed how efforts to improve girls' education had been stymied by environmental degradation. Deforestation and erosion led to economic stress within households, and girls were consequently kept out of school to help at home.

1 *The State of India's Environment 1984-1985*: The Second Citizen's Report, Centre for Science and Environment, New Delhi, 1985. **2** http://www.inmotionmagazine.com/global/vshiva3.html#Anchor-Women-3800 **3** 'Water: every drop counts', *New Internationalist*, no 354, March 2003. **4** Sharon Lamwaka, *No Way Out for Uganda's Chronically Poor?* Panos Features, June 2003. **5** B Agarwal, 'The Gender and Environment Debate', in Keil Roger (ed), *Political ecology: global and local*, Routledge, 1998. **6** Theo Colburn, www.wwf.org **7** 'Pick your poison: the pesticide scandal', *New Internationalist*, no 323, May 2000. **8** See www.pan-international.org Paraquat is one of the 12 dangerous pesticides listed by the Pesticide Action Network. **9** V Arumugam, Teneganita and Pesticides Action Network Asia Pacific, *Victims without voice, a study of women pesticide workers in Malaysia*, www.pan.org **10** *Justice for All: promoting environmental justice in South Asia*, Panos South Asia, August 2002, www.panos.org.np **11** Terry Cannon, 'Gender and climate hazards in Bangladesh', in Rachel Masika (ed), *Gender Development and Climate Change*, Oxfam, 2002. **12** Valerie Nelson, Kate Meadows, Terry Cannon, John Morton and Adrienne Martin, 'Uncertain predictions, invisible impacts and the need to mainstream gender in climate change adaptations', in Rachel Masika (ed), *Gender Development and Climate Change*, Oxfam 2002. **13** *Justice for All: promoting environmental justice in South Asia*, Panos South Asia, August 2002, www.panos.org.np **14** Quoted in *High Stakes: the future for mountain societies*, Panos, May 2002. **15** http://www.diversewomen.org/Issues.htm **16** N Wamykonya and M Skutsch 'COP6: The gender issue forgotten?' in *Energia News*, vol 4 no 1, March 2001. **17** *ENERGIA News*, vol 5 no 4, 2002. **18** 'Differences and similarities: a North-South Comparative Analysis', in *ENERGIA News*, Vol 5 no 4, 2002. **19** 'Gender and Environment: a delicate balance between profit and loss', NEDA, 1997. **20** V Johnson, J Hill and E Ivan Smith, *Listening to Smaller Voices: Children in an environment of change*, Action Aid, 1995.

6 Power, politics and the law

There are more women in politics than ever before, though the numbers are still small. And this is beginning to have an effect on legislation about women's rights.

I think I became a leader because I was angry, and also because at times I felt so impotent, because we women don't speak up.

Emerenciana, local women's leader, Mexico[1]

YOU WOULD NEVER know when looking at a line-up of world leaders, but the greatest improvements in women's status over the last 10 years have been in acquiring a greater share of seats in parliament. This revolution has happened mainly where special measures have been taken to increase numbers, as in Mozambique, where women now hold 30 per cent of the seats. They are not related to the relative 'development' of a country – at 12 per cent, the US has a lower share of women in power than 38 countries in the South.

In Brazil, the Mayor of Sâo Paulo, Marta Suplicy, feels the positive effects of these changes: 'The 21st century is ours, no doubt. I don't think, even in a *machista* country like Brazil, being a woman today is something that goes against you.'[2]

But it is important to remember just how recent these changes have been. In Switzerland women only gained the vote in 1971 – 123 years later than men. In Kuwait, women still can't vote. Nine countries have given women the vote only since 1980. In South Africa white women were allowed to vote in 1931, but Indian and 'colored' women not until 1984, black women not before 1994.[3]

So perhaps it is not so surprising that only 12 countries have achieved the benchmark of 30-per-cent representation set in 1995 in the Platform for Action from the UN Women's conference in Beijing – Sweden, Denmark, Germany, Finland, Norway, Iceland, the Netherlands, South Africa, Costa Rica, Argentina, Mozambique, and, most recently, Rwanda. In all these countries there were legal or voluntary quotas – something that seems to be the key, at least initially, to increasing women's share of seats.

Rwanda beats Sweden into second place

Results of the elections in Rwanda have put the country at the top of the world ranking of women in national parliaments. Women now make up 48.8 per cent of the National Assembly, beating longstanding leader, Sweden, into second place. ■

http://www.ipu.org/english/pressdoc/gen176.htm

In 22 countries women's share of seats in parliament actually fell. In the 2002 *Progress of the World's Women*, UNIFEM notes: 'Particularly disappointing were two cases in which a return to democracy was accompanied by a reduction in women's representation. In Nigeria women's share of seats fell to a very disappointing 3.2 per cent. In Indonesia women's share fell from 11.4 per cent to only 8 per cent.' But in three countries in Eastern Europe – Bulgaria, Poland and the Former Yugoslav Republic of Macedonia – where representation had fallen after the transition to a market economy and the collapse of the Soviet bloc, it rose again to 26.2 per cent, 21.0 per cent and 17.5 per cent respectively.

But trumpeting the many achievements cannot hide the fact that in 2002 women still only accounted for an average of 15.1 per cent of parliamentary seats. The overall increase in numbers since 1995 has been 0.5 per cent per year. 'At that rate, it would take 50 years to get the balance right!' says the 50/50 Campaign, set up in 2000 by the Women's Environment and

Women in Parliament

Women's share of seats in national parliaments, selected countries, October 2003

The range here is enormous; from 2.4% in Egypt to 48.8% in Rwanda – it is not always the richest countries that rank the highest.

Country	Percentage
Rwanda	48.8
Sweden	45.3
Denmark	38.0
Cuba	36.0
Costa Rica	35.1
Mozambique	30.0
South Africa	29.8
New Zealand	28.3
Vietnam	27.3
Bulgaria	26.2
East Timor	26.1
Australia	25.3
Uganda	24.7
China	20.2
Britain	17.9
US	14.3
Tunisia	11.5
India	8.8
Brazil	8.6
Indonesia	8.0
Egypt	2.4

Inter-Parliamentary Union, March 2003 http://www.ipu.org/wmn-e/classif.htm

Development Organization to lobby for equal representation for women and men in parliaments around the world by 2005. Since it began, the 50/50 campaign has been adopted by 154 organizations in 45 countries.

Women are also under-represented at senior levels in all professions – from the United Nations to trade unions and business.

At city and municipal level, women are still in the minority – 1 per cent in Greece, 6 per cent in Brazil, 7 per cent in the Philippines, 26 per cent in New Zealand and 27 per cent in England and Wales. A number of countries reserve seats for women at local level – in India, 33 per cent of seats on village and

A first for Wales

In April 2003 the Welsh Assembly became the first legislative body in the world to be made up of equal numbers of men and women. In the 60-strong Assembly, which was created in 1999 following devolution, there are 30 men and 30 women. And at the highest level, women are even dominant. The new cabinet has five women and four men.

But before 1997 Wales had only ever had four women Members of the British Parliament. How was this all achieved? According to Julie Morgan, Labour MP for Cardiff North and a key campaigner in the battle for equal representation for women, there is a long tradition of Welsh women who have been active behind the scenes in politics, but because of the male working-class culture and trade-union politics that dominated Wales, they found it hard to come through the party hierarchy.

With devolution and the creation of the new assembly in 1999, women like Morgan realized they had an ideal opportunity to achieve a more representative gender balance. But the only way to do it at that stage was through positive action. A number of influential women decided to argue for a mechanism known as 'twinning' – pairing two constituencies, asking party members to vote for one man and one woman, and allowing the constituencies to sort out between them which area got which candidate. 'It was an extremely difficult policy to get through,' says Morgan. 'We had very strong resistance from some ministers at the time. It was seen as taking democracy from the party.' The debate became divisive, but the policy was finally passed by a tiny majority at the Welsh Labour Party's 1997 conference in Swansea.

Katherine Rake, director of the Fawcett Society, which campaigns for fairer political representation for women, says: 'What the Welsh experience shows is that positive-action mechanisms work. You can transform the political landscape if you're committed to introducing positive measures... If Wales can lead the way, why not Westminster as well?'

The Assembly's biggest achievement may be in changing the way that women are perceived in public life in Wales, suggests Helen Mary Jones, Plaid Cymru regional Member of the Assembly for Mid and West Wales. She hopes it will encourage more women to come forward for public appointments. 'Having parity is going to send such a strong signal in public life in Wales and beyond. We have gone from being a bit of an equal-opportunities backwater to being an equal-opportunities star. It's fantastic. We're all so proud.' ∎

Sally Weale, *The Guardian*, 9 May 2003.

Profile: Hiteni Shekudja

Hiteni Shekudja was elected to represent women from her village in the committee of traditional leaders in 1996, after the President of Namibia had called on traditional authorities to include more women in their structures. Before this she had held a number of other leadership positions in her community. 'I also like straightforward talking, and maybe that's another quality that people valued when they elected me as their leader,' she says, with laughter in her eyes.

She believes that women's leadership is needed to make sure that the new laws bringing about gender equality are actually implemented. She says that women should become more involved in decision making at all levels of society and see themselves as leaders in their own right. She firmly believes that women have the skills and capacity to make good leaders, and hopes that one of her daughters will step into her shoes as head woman when the time comes. Chances may not be bad, with five of her six children being girls.

Her message to girls is to look after themselves well and study hard so that they can eventually earn their own income and not become dependent on men. At the same time she expects boys to grow up acknowledging and accepting the equal human rights of girls and women.

Would she consider leadership at the regional or national level in the future? She certainly would! Come elections, Hiteni Shekudja stands ready to bridge the gap between traditional and modern structures of leadership, and to help close the gender gap to achieve 50/50, 'because it will be better to share experiences with the people who understand your problems'. ■

Cover story, *Sister Namibia*, Vol 13 no 5 & 6, September-December 2001, published in English and Oshindonga.

district councils, resulting in nearly a million elected women leaders. However, a great deal of manipulation takes place. Many women are put up like political puppets while their husbands pull the strings.

In Tanzania 20 per cent of national seats and 25 per cent of local-government seats are reserved for women. In South America 12 countries have adopted laws establishing a minimum level of 20 to 40 per cent for women's participation in national elections.

One of the difficulties for a woman of taking on such public positions is that very often the long hours involved take them away from home and family, and there may be no-one at home to do the work. Some women have decided that it is not worth it: of the 108 women who have appeared on the US *Fortune 500* list of top earners over the past five years, at least 20 have left their prestigious positions – most of their own voli-tion, like former Pepsi-Cola North America CEO Brenda Barnes (who moved home to Illinois to focus on her family) and former Fidelity Personal

Empty words or real commitment?

A review of the resolutions on women by international conferences

2001 The World Conference on Racism promised to 'incorporate a gender perspective in all programs of action against racism, racial discrimination, xenophobia and related intolerance'.

2001 The UN AIDS Conference (whose motto was: 'Healthy women, healthy world') promised to: 'Give priority to the health of women, and, above all, to make sure they have the freedom, the power and the knowledge to take decisions affecting their own lives and those of their families.' (Footnote speech)

2000 Optional Protocol to the Women's Convention For the first time, this allows any woman whose human rights have been violated under the Convention to take her complaint to the UN.

2000 The UN Millennium Declaration committed its signatories to the goal of 'gender equality and empowerment of women', saying that the achievement of this was critical to the achievement of all the other goals.

1996 The World Food Summit acknowledged 'the fundamental contribution to food security by women, particularly in rural areas of developing countries, and the need to ensure equality between men and women'.

1996 The World Conference on Human Settlements (Habitat II) made a commitment to 'enhancing the role of women'.

1995 The Fourth UN World Conference on Women, Beijing The Platform for Action mentions 'rights' approximately 500 times and calls for the protection of a wide range of women's rights. It is an important document, used by women's groups and governments to work on gender equality.

1995 The World Summit on Social Development, Copenhagen Women's organizations persuaded governments to look at the negative impacts on women of macro-economic policies, especially structural adjustment.

Investments president Gail McGovern (now a marketing professor at Harvard Business School).

Legal rights

Leadership gives women the possibility of making changes in the laws so that they favor women's rights – although, again, there are fewer women than men at the top of the legal profession. Such laws cannot change things overnight, but, as feminist lawyers note,

1994 The International Conference on Population and Development, Cairo after much fraught debate, introduced a 20-year policy agenda that is shaping reproductive and sexual health programs and policies around the world. Women's groups succeeded in moving the focus from the reduction of population growth to women's sexual and reproductive health and rights.

1993 The World Conference on Human Rights, Vienna stated clearly for the first time that: 'The human rights of women and of the girl-child are an inalienable, integral and indivisible part of universal human rights. The full and equal participation of women in political, civil, economic, social and cultural life, at the national, regional and international levels, and the eradication of all forms of discrimination on grounds of sex are priority objectives of the international community.'

1993 The Declaration on the Elimination of Violence Against Women defines such violence as 'any act of gender-based violence that results in, or is likely to result in physical, sexual or psychological harm or suffering to women including threats of such acts, coercion or arbitrary deprivation of liberty, whether occurring in public or in private.'

1991 The Rio Declaration on Environment and Development states: 'Women have a vital role in environmental management and development. Their full participation is therefore essential to achieve sustainable development.' Initial drafts had only two references to women; a lobby from women's groups and others ensured that the final document had 170, and a chapter on women's role in the environment.

1990 The World Conference on Education committed itself to 'Education for All' and set targets for gender equality in education.

1979 The International Convention on the Elimination of All Forms of Discrimination against Women (CEDAW) was agreed. This is also known as the Women's Convention and is, essentially, an international bill of rights for women. ∎

Targets for women's empowerment at international women's conferences

Lists of targets and international declarations may not seem very exciting, but they mark important benchmarks that women nationally can use to argue for women's rights. Each of the conferences here made commitments to achieve certain rights for women by a certain date – those commitments are shown with a tick.

	UN Women's Conference in Cairo 1990	UN Social Summit in Copenhagen 1995	UN Women's Conference in Beijing 1995	UN Millennium Summit 2000
By the year 2000... Life expectancy not less than 60 years in any country		✓		
Universal access to basic education and 80% of children to complete primary education	✓	✓	✓	
Gender equality for girls in primary education			✓	
Maternal mortality reduced by one half of 1990 level	✓	✓	✓	
By the year 2005...				
Close the gender gap in primary and secondary education	✓	✓	✓	✓ (preferably by 2005)
Improve the ratio of literate females to males among 15 to 24-year-olds				✓

	UN Women's Conference in Cairo 1990	UN Social Summit in Copenhagen 1995	UN Women's Conference in Beijing 1995	UN Millennium Summit 2000
Remove all program-related barriers to family planning	✓			
Countries with highest maternal mortality rates aim for below 125 deaths per 1,000 births; medium rates aim for below 100	✓			
By the year 2015...				
Provide universal primary education in all countries	✓	✓	✓	✓
Reproductive healthcare accessible to all through primary healthcare systems	✓	✓	✓	
Gender equality in education	✓			✓
Reduce maternal mortality rates by a further 50 %	✓			✓ (by 75% since 1990)
Life expectancy greater than 70 in countries with highest mortality rates	✓			
Eradicate extreme poverty and hunger		✓		✓ halve proportion living on $1 a day
Increase the proportion of seats held by women in national parliaments			✓	✓ (30%)
Reduce the spread of HIV/AIDS among 15-24 year old women				✓

they are a starting point which women can use to their advantage. 'Changes in laws, civil codes, systems of property rights, control over our bodies, labor codes and the social and legal institutions that underwrite male control and privilege are essential if [we] women are to attain justice in society,' says the women's organization DAWN (Development Alternatives for a New Era).[4]

The last 15 years have seen many international legal instruments enacted that apply directly to women, and many more that are not ostensibly about women but which have a number of relevant clauses. Each has built on the previous one – the World Food Summit, for example, reaffirmed its commitment to the Beijing Plan of Action. And they have led to a string of international targets on gender equality.

All treaties have independent supervisory bodies that monitor implementation, encourage compliance and offer guidance. The documents – such as a Plan or Program of Action – which emerge from each conference help to develop new international standards, assist in the implementation of human-rights law at national levels and set benchmarks for policy makers. Though not legally binding upon states, the action programs of key conferences in the 1990s have provided a useful and practical tool to develop policy.

However, the current backlash has made women's groups cautious of further conferences and commitments. A statement from the women's organization DAWN (Development Alternatives for a New Era) in April 2003 explains why:

'Contrary to the relatively open environment for such advances that existed during the 1990s, the first decade of the 21st century confronts us with the extreme social conservatism, aggressive unilateralism, and support for militarism of the Bush Administration, and the worsening of fundamentalist trends elsewhere as well. In such a context, it is very

The Women's Convention

The International Convention on the Elimination of All Forms of Discrimination against Women (CEDAW) requires states to eliminate 'discrimination against women in the enjoyment of all civil, political, economic and cultural rights'. It also establishes programmatic measures for states to pursue in achieving equality between women and men.

Currently, 170 countries – more than two-thirds of the members of the UN – have ratified the Convention, committing themselves to a legally binding international treaty, including participation in a country-by-country reporting process. An additional 97 countries have signed the treaty, binding themselves to do nothing in contravention of its terms.

However, it has been a Convention with few teeth. Enforcement has been difficult, and although it represents a strong statement about women's human rights, in practice it is weak and often ignored. Signatories to the Women's Convention have made more reservations to its provisions than to any other UN convention.

This was why, after four years of negotiations, the 43rd session of the Commission on the Status of Women adopted an agreed version of the Optional Protocol to CEDAW in March 1999. The negotiation of the Protocol had been controversial and the final version was ultimately a compromise between the strong views of negotiating Nation States. It came into force in December 2000, by which time 13 states had ratified it and 62 had signed it. Amnesty International hailed the Optional Protocol as 'a landmark for women's human rights'. It brings CEDAW onto an equal footing with other international human-rights instruments.

The US, on the other hand, is among the few countries that have not ratified CEDAW. The Bush Administration initially identified CEDAW as a 'Category II Treaty', meaning it was 'generally desirable and should be approved'. But, reportedly in response to howls of protest from Bush's ultra-right-wing supporters, the State Department changed its tune, calling the treaty 'vague'. It also indicated that it wants the Justice Department to review the treaty before the Senate votes on it.

Scripps Howard News Service, 'US retreats on UN pact backing women's rights', Lisa Hoffman, July 22, 2002. ■

important to protect the gains made for women's human rights through careful and considered action. We believe, in this context, it is imperative that there NOT be any international or regional inter-govern-

mental meetings that in any way involve or may lead
to official negotiations.'[5]

The law and the courts

At a regional level there have been meetings to follow
up the women's rights aspects of the Women's
Convention in all areas and on all continents. Many of
these have been organized by women's groups who
have also carried out their own research to find out
what impact international action plans have had.

At a national level, women have used international
laws, in particular the Women's Convention, to lobby
their governments to change national laws. One effective way of doing this is to press for the inclusion of
women's human rights in national constitutions. They
then become the baseline for governmental obligations.

The way in which this happens varies from country
to country; some make ratified treaties part of national
law. Others include explicit guarantees of gender
equality. For example, while the 1986 African Charter
on Human and People's Rights does not specifically
apply to women, national courts in Botswana, Tanzania
and Zimbabwe are using it to make their governments
change laws that are discriminatory against women.

In Colombia, organizations including 'feminists and
women's organizations' were invited to put proposals
for the reform of the constitution. They decided to
come together in a single umbrella group which soon
grew to include more than 70 groups from across the
country. It called itself the Women and Constitution
Network and today the Colombian Constitution
contains some of the most 'detailed and substantive
guarantees of women's human rights in the world'.[6]

These are not just 'paper equality' statements, but
oblige the government actively to promote the conditions needed to make them real and effective, and to
adopt affirmative action if necessary. There is also an
enforcement mechanism that individual women can
use, via a Constitutional Court.

The Colombian Constitutional Court

This court has made a number of important decisions involving women's human rights. It has recognized the principle that women's domestic work has real economic value. When called upon to determine a woman's property rights after the death of her common-law husband, the court recognised her domestic work as having contributed to the acquisition and improvement of their home. In another decision, the Court ordered a high school to reaccept a girl who had been expelled for becoming pregnant. In 1993, the Court released a decision regarding the treatment of women prisoners that relied explicitly on the Women's Convention. A challenge was brought over prison regulations that required women prisoners to be fitted with an IUD or take contraceptives prior to conjugal visits but did not make men wear condoms on similar visits. The court ordered that the prison system cease enforcing this regulation, as it violated the constitution's protection against sex discrimination, its guarantee of reproductive and family rights, and the obligation placed on the State to provide women special assistance and protection around pregnancy and birth. The court also found that the regulation was in violation of the Women's Convention. ∎

www.unifem.org

In South Africa, after the end of apartheid, a coalition of women's groups, academics, women politicians and women's trade-union groups presented a charter of women's rights, as a result of which the South African Constitution contains a number of significant provisions guaranteeing women's equality. 'Non-sexism' is listed with 'non-racism' as one of the State's fundamental values.

In Africa, common and customary law has generally discriminated against women. For example, in some countries women are not allowed to inherit, own or sell land, or to pass their nationality on to their children. Courts in countries like Tanzania are beginning to address this problem – nationality laws have been reformed in Mauritius and Zimbabwe and also in other non-African countries such as Costa Rica, Italy, Jamaica, Lebanon and Portugal.

Sexual harassment in India

In 1992 a group of women's non-governmental organizations (NGOs) brought a petition to the Supreme Court of India. Their petition was motivated by the gang rape of a social worker by her own colleagues in a village in Rajasthan, and the failure of local officials to investigate. However, the problem the NGOs asked the court to address was much broader: there were no laws in India that prohibited sexual harassment in the workplace. Relying on provisions of the Indian Constitution, on the Women's Convention and its Committee's General Recommendation 19 on violence against women, the NGOs argued that the court should draft a law to compensate for the Indian Parliament's inaction.

The legal question the court had to resolve was whether the State actually had an obligation to protect women from sexual harassment. The Constitution prohibited discrimination on the basis of sex, and guaranteed just and humane conditions of work, but it didn't refer explicitly to sexual harassment. The court decided in August 1997 that by ratifying CEDAW and by making official commitments at the 1995 Beijing world conference on women, India had endorsed the international standard of women's human rights. According to this standard, gender equality requires protection from sexual harassment.

The court drew up a set of national guidelines, including detailed requirements for processing sexual harassment complaints, that will bind private and public employers until the Government passes suitable legislation. They include a definition of sexual harassment: 'Sexual harassment includes such unwelcome sexually determined behaviour (whether directly or by implication) as: a) physical contact and advances; b) a demand or request for sexual favors; c) sexually colored remarks; d) showing pornography; e) any other unwelcome physical, verbal or non-verbal conduct of a sexual nature.' ■

www.unifem.org

At the grassroots

Many of these changes in the law, based on international legislation, have come about through pressure from women's non-governmental organizations. But at the grassroots many women have no idea about laws, national or international, and no knowledge of how to use them.

A number of organizations is working to change this. Some, like the Association of Black Women Lawyers of New Jersey, were set up to ensure that

Women and the law in Mexico

Many Mexican women know little about the law. This was the conclusion of research undertaken by SEDEPAC (Sevicio, Desarollo y Paz, AC), an organization founded in 1983 to support the activities and education of groups searching for solutions to poverty and marginalization. They established that in Mexico:

- 'The majority of women living in poor neighborhoods have no knowledge of existing laws, and even less of their own rights. They feel totally powerless to defend themselves at home or in a legal court. They do not have in their hands the instruments to search for solutions.
- 'There is an appalling lack of alternative legal services for women in Mexico.
- 'The existing laws have to be changed, reformed and/or enforced; in order to do this, women must be informed of the law in its existing form, if they are to push for changes.
- 'The legal system is authoritarian and conservative; therefore it helps to maintain cultural and social stereotypes.'

To counter these problems they organized a series of workshops. Margarita Fernanadez, a 24-year-old beautician who did not finish secondary school, was one of those who attended. She works in a grassroots organization with young people in her spare time.

'When the invitation for the workshop arrived, I thought "this is important" because, since I started participating in the popular urban struggle, I have seen a lot of conflicts and personal problems affecting both men and women. Let me give you some examples: police violence in our poor neighborhoods, the frequency of rapes in our streets, men constantly beating their wives.

'Before the workshop, I could do nothing... At the workshop we studied the Penal and Civil codes [and] the Constitution. We have... the legal jargon we need to talk to the judges when we are defending a teenager... Just recently we went to Toluca [near Mexico City] to defend a *compañera* who had been raped, and what we had learned worked! The workshop helped because it gave us theory as well as practical tools.' ■

Caroline Sweetman (ed), *Women and Rights*, Oxfam UK and Ireland, 1998.

there were increasing numbers of female lawyers who can improve the quality of the legal services for women. Others, like Women and Law in Southern

Africa and Women and Law and Development in Africa, lobby their governments to ratify international human-rights conventions and incorporate them into the laws of the land.

Women need both the theory and the practical tools to be able to use legislation to their advantage.

1 Caroline Sweetman (ed), *Women and Rights*, Oxfam UK and Ireland, 1998. **2** Interviewed for TVE *City Life* program. **3** Joni Seager, *The Atlas of Women*, The Women's Press, 2003. **4** DAWN 1987, 81, quoted in Caroline Sweetman (ed), *Women and Rights*, Oxfam UK and Ireland, 1998. **5** www.dawn.org **6** www.UNIFEM.org

7 Literacy and learning – make education your husband

Women's and girls' education does not just help those concerned; it is key to a country's economic development. But women still make up two-thirds of the world's illiterate people. And progress is painfully slow.

'Make education your husband,' my mother used to say, 'he will never tire of you. If I was growing up during these times of yours, my child, I would not bother getting married. I would just make sure I got an education and worked for myself.'

Sindiwe Magona, South African writer[1]

IT MAY SEEM obvious, but for women to be able make the changes that are needed, they need to be able to read and write. While women's dis-empowerment at so many levels is due not just to lack of education, simply having the tools of literacy and communication makes a big difference. And educating women has huge benefits for the whole community, as well as for women themselves:

- It has been shown to increase women's productivity, raising output and reducing poverty.
- It promotes gender equality within households, improves women's ability to make decisions, reduces the number of babies they have and improves maternal health.
- It supports greater participation of girls and women in leadership and decision-making roles.
- Educated women do a better job caring for children, increasing children's chances of surviving to become healthier and better educated.
- It has lasting benefits to future generations and for society as a whole.[2]

And yet targets to close the gender gap in education by 2005 and for women's literacy and universal basic education by 2015 are unlikely to be met in many countries. Illiteracy may even increase during the early years of this century, after declining during the 1990s. Conflict, war and AIDS are all affecting children's – and girls' – education. In Swaziland, for example, it is estimated that three to four teachers die every week from AIDS.[3]

Today, 862 million adults – one sixth of the world's population – are still illiterate. Two-thirds of these are women. Most are from the poorest sectors of society and have never attended school, or only for a brief period.

There are still an estimated 140 million illiterate young people in the world, of whom more than half – 86 million – are young women. In countries where less than 50 per cent of young women are literate, progress is slow. UNESCO projects that, if current growth rates continue, there will still be an estimated 67 million young women (out of 107 million young people) who are illiterate by 2015.

Of the 132 million children who do not attend school, two-thirds are girls. In low-income countries, girls tend either to drop out from school earlier than boys or not go at all.

Missing out
- 569 million women cannot read or write
- 86 million young women are illiterate
- 87 million girls do not attend school

The good news
The Dakar World Education Forum in 2000 pledged to ensure that by 2015 all children – and particularly girls, children in difficult circumstances and ethnic minorities – would have access to free and compulsory

Time needed to achieve 95-per-cent female youth literacy rate at current rates of change

These are the countries with the lowest literacy levels – most of them still have many years to go until nearly all young women are even able to read.

	Female youth literacy rate (%) 2002	Average annual rate of change (%) 1988-2002	Number of years needed to reach 95%
Niger	14.9	4.1	45
Bangladesh	41.4	2.1	40
Mauritania	41.8	2.1	38
Burkina Faso	25.7	5.2	25
Pakistan	44.2	3.2	24
Benin	35.8	3.8	23
Senegal	44.3	3.3	23
Mozambique	49.2	3.8	17
Nepal	46.0	4.8	15
Guinea-Bissau	47.4	5.0	14

Progress of Women 2002, UNIFEM

primary education. Gender disparity was to be eliminated by 2005. The conference also set up the UN Girls' Education Initiative in which 13 UN bodies, led by UNICEF, have agreed to work together on a 10-year initiative to help governments meet their commitments to ensure a quality education for girls all over the world.

The UN Literacy Decade began in 2003. There have been many things to celebrate during the past decade as well. Recent figures show that women are gaining access to education and literacy at a faster rate than men. The trend is most evident in Africa, where the percentage of illiterate women over the age of 15 has fallen 6.4 per cent – to 49 per cent – in the last decade. The gap between girls' and boys' enrolments has narrowed too. Girls' enrolment doubled between the mid-1970s and the mid-1990s in Benin, Cape Verde, Chad, Ethiopia, Gambia, Guinea, Guinea-Bissau, Malawi, Mauritania, Nepal, Nigeria, Oman, Senegal and Sierra Leone. East Asia may well achieve the UN Millennium Goal of eliminating gender disparity in education by 2005. Progress has also been good in the Middle East and North Africa, and in South Asia. But in Sub-Saharan Africa progress has been disappointing.

In a number of countries, girls have started to outstrip boys; 48 per cent of countries now have a higher secondary-school enrolment rate for girls than for boys, perhaps because boys leave school for work earlier than girls. In some Northern countries it is boys who are struggling at school amid a culture where learning is not seen as 'cool'. In England, for example, 57 per cent of girls but only 46 per cent of boys gained five or more of the top three grades at the GCSE examination in 2001.

Young women's literacy, 2002

In the North:

- 95 per cent or more of young women are literate

In the rest of the world:

- 61 countries have 95 per cent or more literacy
- 54 countries have between 50 and 95 per cent
- 11 countries have less than 10 per cent.

Why don't girls go to school?

'If you have a situation where women ands girls are discriminated against in society and not all children are in school, it follows almost as night follows day that girls will be kept out of school most,' says Christopher Colclough of the Institute of Development Studies (IDS) at the University of

Sussex, England, who conducted a nine-country research project in sub-Saharan Africa.[4]

Women's status in society has a direct effect on the number of girls attending school. School is often perceived as a lower priority for girls than for boys, especially when parents have to pay and can only afford to send some of their children. In many countries the costs of schooling have risen as part of the privatization of education.

'A lot of girls are dropping out of school or not being sent at all because of the poverty of parents,' says Peninah Mlama, executive director of the Forum for African Women Educationalists (FAWE). 'Traditional cultural attitudes are still very strong, especially in rural areas. The little money parents have to scrounge for sending children to school is seen as too big an investment to risk on the girl child.'[5]

Schools may also be far away, making it more of a problem for girls to get to. Or families prefer to keep girls at home to help with childcare and other chores. In addition, more girls than boys drop out of school. This may be due to discriminatory attitudes, practices and behavior by teachers, parents and community members, and to the fact that there are few female role models. Girls at school may find that the curriculum, teaching methods and even text books have a gender bias which makes them feel uncomfortable. In all the countries where the IDS team conducted their research, they found that teachers believed boys were more intelligent than girls.

In addition, where girls marry early they are not expected to go to school, and girls who fall pregnant may be expelled.

Girls in all countries often face sexual harassment – and worse – at school, but may be afraid to speak out. Sometimes this is because the teacher is the perpetrator. Lack of action on the part of school authorities, even in the most appalling cases, can lead to girls being afraid to go to school, as this South African

13-year old, who had been raped by her classmates, pointed out:

'After the school break, my mom asked me if I wanted to go back to school. I said no. All the people who I thought were my friends had turned against me. And they [the rapists] were still there. I felt disappointed. [Teachers] always told me they were glad to have students like me, that they wished they had more students like me. If they had made the boys leave, I wouldn't have felt so bad about it.'[6]

What can be done?

If more girls are to be educated, schools need to take steps themselves, and measures must also be taken at

---

National action to narrow the gender gap

Governments are taking action to ensure that girls go to school. They include:

Pakistan All primary schools will be co-educational; all new primary schools are required to have ratios of 60 girls to 40 boys and 70 per cent women teachers. Where the number of women teachers is inadequate, age and qualification requirements for them will be relaxed. Special incentives, like monetary incentives, will be used to attract and retain female teachers in rural areas and under-served regions of the country.

Benin School fees for girls will be eliminated in public primary schools in rural areas. A campaign to sensitize parents on gender issues in education will be conducted through the media.

Mauritania An overall strategy with an integrated socio-economic, cultural and institutional approach has been developed to improve girls' participation in education. Incentives include reducing the distance children have to travel to school, increasing the number of women teachers, establishing scholarships for girls, and increasing the number of school canteens.

Niger A 1998 law stipulates: 'The State is committed to identify and remove socio-cultural barriers, pedagogical hurdles and other obstacles which hinder the full development of girls and women in the learning process.' ■

Education for All 2002, UNESCO.

---

government level. Governments are looking at ways of improving gender equality in schools – by increasing the number of women teachers, ensuring that schools are close enough for girls to travel safely, and reducing or eliminating school fees for girls. But there are other problems – waiving school fees does not address the question of how to replace a girl's labor at home or in the fields, nor the bias in some countries against educating daughters.

'Nearly every single policy document mentions girls' education, it's almost as if it is the politically

Community schools in Egypt

In some villages in southern Egypt only 12 girls are enrolled for every 100 boys. Girls' net enrolment rates range from 50 to 70 per cent, while the national average is 90 per cent. The main reasons given for non-attendance were the distance girls had to travel to get to school, and the fact that their parents could not afford to send them.

'We wish all girls, women and men of the village would get an education,' said an elderly man from the village of Helba, 'but we can't afford it, nor can we allow our girls to go to far places on their own.'

But now community schools have come to the area. Communities donate the space, ensure that children come to class and manage the schools themselves through an education committee. The Ministry of Education pays facilitators and provides textbooks. The overall program is the responsibility of UNICEF.

Girls no longer have to travel far to go to school. There are flexible timetables and no hidden costs such as uniforms.

And the teaching is lively. The facilitators – young women from the area who have an intermediate school certificate – adapt the curriculum to local interests with the help of a range of learning guides produced together with facilitators. These are now being used in 3,500 classrooms. The experience of teaching has changed things for the facilitators and children alike; many of the former are declaring that they will only marry a man who allows them to continue teaching and girls of 12 are convincing their parents to postpone marriage until they finish school.

Since the program started in 1992, community schools have reached 6,000 children, and girls' enrollment has reached 70 per cent. ∎

www.unesco.org/courier/2001_05/uk/education2.htm

correct language to use,' says Peninah Mlama. 'But governments don't have the capacity and commitment to really do something.'

'If there is one lesson we have learned, it's that there is no single quick fix, but there are usually two or three actions together that are catalytic,' says Mary Joy Pigozzi, a senior UNICEF education adviser.

Two of the most important are involving parents and communities in schools and improving the quality of education. Pigozzi says that this has to happen through affirmative action that acknowledges how different a girl's situation may be from her brother's. 'You have to understand that girls may get less protein than boys, that communities raise girls to have different expectations of themselves. Then you have to look at the quality of the learning environment to address issues such as safety and sexual harassment, and the whole teaching-learning process.'[7]

Literacy

Women's literacy is also vital for any kind of national development. There are a number of programs which promote literacy alongside a range of other measures to help women gain confidence and economic independence.

The Dhaka Ahsania Mission is one such organization that has been changing women's lives across Asia. Six years ago it started classes in a village in western Bangladesh. It was a big step to take. The women were not allowed out; they could not meet strangers even if they visited their homes, and most had never been to school.

'By tradition we could not even pronounce our husband's name,' said Hira Akhtar. When she asked permission to go to classes from her husband, who could barely pen a signature himself, he threw up his hands. 'What will happen by reading all these books?' he asked.

But these were not ordinary books and the classes

were not like at a school. The Dhaka Ahsania Mission opened membership to representatives of the 250 poorest families out of the 311 families in the village – those earning less than 2,700 taka ($47) a month – and ensured that 75 per cent of them were the most disadvantaged members of those families: women.

The classes concentrate on literacy, numeracy and subjects relevant to the learners' lives. More than 50,000 of the poorest people will this year be using their self-learning guides to learn how to read and write.

A crucial factor in the success of the centres is that each is run by a committee of members and comes together to discuss issues concerning the whole village.

A survey of Rogaghurampur, a 100-household village of 450 people in Jessore district, where 63 families had been active members since 1998, has documented the dramatic changes since the centre began its work. By December 2002 the percentage of literate families had more than doubled from 30 to 65; the number using latrines and fuel efficient ovens had soared; the practice of marrying children off at 13 or younger had been wiped out, with knock-on effects on the number and spacing of pregnancies; the role of women in decision-making and earning an income had been completely transformed; and the percentage of girls going to school jumped from 30 to 100.

Now Hira's husband asks her to borrow books for him to read.

'In the early days many of the women who returned home late from the classes were beaten. Men didn't think we should leave the house for anything,' said Hira. 'But now attitudes have changed completely. The status of women has been raised a lot. Now if someone says your wife needs to go for training in Dhaka, the husband will gladly agree.'[8]

There are many projects, like this one, that teach women to read and help girls to get to school and stay there. But they also need training – vocational, practical and on-the-job: an area where women and girls often miss out and which affects their ability to improve their work, earn more money and develop their potential.

But as long as poverty and cultural norms that favor boys exist, and the political will is lacking, it will take a long time for any targets to be reached. In the meantime female babies will be born, develop into young women, bear children and die without ever seeing the inside of a schoolroom.

1 Sindiwe Magona is a black South African who now lives in the US. This quote is from her article in 'Back to the drawing board: the war on education', *New Internationalist*, no 248, October 1993. **2** United Nations Girls' Education Initiative. **3** *Unesco Courier*, 2001. www.unesco.org/courier/2001_05/uk/education.htm **4** *Progress of Women 2002*, UNIFEM. **5** *Unesco Courier*, 2001. www.unesco.org/courier/2001_05/uk/education.htm **6** *Unesco Courier*, 2001 www.unesco.org/courier/2001_05/uk/education.htm **7** *Scared at School: Sexual Violence against Girls in South African Schools*, Human Rights Watch, 2001. **8** *Unesco Courier*, 2001. www.unesco.org/courier/2001_05/uk/education.htm

8 Double jeopardy: violence against women

The last century was the most violent in history. Much of the violence was against women, both in war and peace. Violence is used to control women, and it takes many forms, from rape and murder to female genital cutting. But men and women have been taking action against such violence – and sometimes succeeded.

'Significant numbers of the world's population are routinely subject to torture, starvation, terrorism, humiliation, mutilation and even murder simply because they are female. Crimes such as these against any other group would be recognized as a civil and political emergency.'

Feminist academics Charlotte Bunch and Roxanna Carillo[1]

Intimate partner violence

SEXUAL, PHYSICAL AND psychological violence causes as much of a burden of ill health and death among women aged 15 to 44 as cancer – and more than malaria and traffic accidents combined. Most of this violence is committed by someone the women know, and often in their own homes.

Boom time for rapists

We are living in a boom time for rape. Last year women reported 27 per cent more rapes than in the year before. At the same time, convictions have plummeted to a record-breaking low: only 5.8 per cent of reported rapes end with a conviction, down from 7.5 per cent in 1999 and 33 per cent in 1977. Not just a boom time for rape, then – also a boom time for rapists. There has never been a better time to rape and get away with it. ∎

Katherine Viner, *The Guardian*, 2 August 2003.

Double jeopardy

In 48 population-based surveys around the world, between 10 and 90 per cent of women reported being physically assaulted by an intimate partner at some point in their lives. In some countries, one in four women report sexual violence by an intimate partner, and up to a third of girls report forced sexual initiation.[2]

This is true in the poor world and the rich one. In Peshawar, Pakistan:

'One woman was not allowed out of her house for any reason, not even to fetch water for cooking or drinking. This task was usually performed by her son or other male relatives. One day when her son was sick and no other male relatives were around she decided to sneak out to fetch water. Unfortunately she ran into her husband on the way back from the water points and he said: "Now I have seen you, so other men must have seen and tomorrow my name will be dust." He beat her with a stick. One of the women from the area saw this and quickly ran to the scene with a blanket. She covered the woman to stop her husband beating her and dressed the woman's wounds, because she knew she would not be able to leave the house to receive medical assistance.'[3]

Sexual violence crosses race, class and religious divides.

In the US a woman is beaten every 18 minutes. Domestic violence is the leading cause of injury among women of reproductive age. Between 22 and 35 per cent of women who visit emergency rooms are there for that reason.[4]

In Peru 70 per cent of all crimes reported to the police involve women beaten by their husbands.[5]

In Russia one woman in five is regularly beaten by her partner.[6]

In the Middle East 'honor killings' – when relatives kill a woman for alleged adultery or sexual misconduct – are still common.

In India and Bangladesh women are killed or

burned with acid for not bringing enough dowry into their husband's family when they marry.

Domestic violence and the law

In the 1990s many countries enacted domestic-violence legislation. Its content varied:

- Some legislation was limited to civil law, providing routes to protection orders for the first time (Finland, Spain) or dealing explicitly with child contact in the context of domestic violence (New Zealand).
- Some extended the ways protection orders and police powers could be used (Austria, Ireland).
- Some linked civil and criminal processes (Cyprus, Mexico, Nicaragua, some states in the US).
- Some created new criminal offences or changed the status of assaults in the home (Belgium, France, Spain, Sweden).
- Some was in the form of 'integrated law', referring to both legal powers and state responsibilities in terms of funding services and setting up monitoring/prevention projects under a system of funding from the state (Cyprus, Austria, Denmark, Finland, Sweden). ∎

Liz Kelly, *Specific Domestic Violence Legislation: Examples and Advantages*, January 2001. www.domesticviolencedata.org/3_ notice/forum/liz_legn.htm

Only 45 countries have legislation protecting women against domestic violence, and many of these laws are not regularly enforced. In Cambodia, women's organizations are working with lawyers to revise the draft law on domestic violence that is expected to come into force later this year. There are posters telling stories in cartoon style, proclaiming that 'Domestic violence is against the law'. 'After five years of work, people have begun to understand that domestic violence is not a private issue,' says Hor Phally, Director of the Project Against Domestic Violence.[7]

Murdered women

- In Brazil 72 per cent of murdered women were killed by a relative or friend.
- In 1999 in the US 23 women a week were murdered by people they knew; 74 per cent of murders of women occurred after the woman left the relationship.
- In Britain two women a week are murdered by their partners.
- In India an estimated 98 women a week are murdered by their husband or husband's family.
- In Bangladesh 50 per cent of all murders are husbands killing their wives.
- In Russia 269 women a week were killed by their husbands or partners in the mid-1990s. ■

Joni Seager, *The Atlas of Women: an economic, social and political survey*, The Women's Press, third edition, 2003.

States have tended to adopt a passive attitude when confronted by cases of violations of women's rights, especially when they occur within the home. What happens between a man and a woman, especially when she is his wife, is seen as a 'private' matter. Even when laws against domestic violence exist, most fail to protect victims or to punish perpetrators. Often police are also complicit, and the law becomes very hard to enforce.

Passing laws to criminalize violence against women is an important way to redefine the limits of acceptable behavior. In recent years women have increasingly been using the law to seek redress.

Men against violence against women

But the law is not the only factor. Men are the perpetrators of these crimes. Many societies condone violence against women if it is committed by her husband. Changing this means a fundamental review of the relationships between men and women and the unequal power that exists between them. 'Educating boys and men to view women as valuable partners in life, in the development of a society and in the attainment of peace, are just as important as taking legal steps to protect women's human rights,' says the United Nations.[8]

The need to involve men in the gender-equality movement was first explicitly articulated in the Cairo Plan of Action on Population and Development. Since then it has been recognized as a powerful strategy to enhance the participation of men. As (most) males are the beneficiaries of gender inequalities, they hold the keys to eliminating them. Men have the economic, moral, political, religious and social responsibility to combat all forms of gender discrimination.

Men against sexual assault

A code of conduct drawn up by men at the University of Rochester in the US

- Don't have sex with a person against their will. Make sure that the sex you are having is consensual.
- Take responsibility for your own actions.
- Watch out for your buddies and your friends when you go out to make sure that none of you get into bad situations.
- Communicate – talk with your partner to make sure that you are both on the same page.
- Talk with your friends – discuss issues such as rape and sexual assault, try to clear up any misconceptions or misunderstandings you may have.
- Educate yourself and those around you about sexual assault.
- Support organizations which fight to decrease the occurrence of sexual assault and rape.
- Don't condone rape jokes, speak up when you hear one and say that it is offensive.
- Believe what people tell you if they have been raped or know someone who has.
- Don't assume that women want your protection; however, offer it to them and be there for them if they do want it.
- Organize or join a group of men at your school, workplace or just with your friends to work against rape and sexual assault. ■

http://sa.rochester.edu/masa/

Double jeopardy

Several men's groups have been set up specifically to do this. The White Ribbon campaign, where men wear a white ribbon to show their opposition to violence against women, has taken off in Canada, Brazil and a number of European countries.[9] On Human Rights Day, 10 December 2002, 150,000 people in Siberia marched against violence against women. The Campaign has inspired the first men's groups against violence against women in China. [10]

Female genital cutting

Other practices can also be considered a form of violence against women. Female genital cutting (FGC) is the most obvious of these. Between 100 and 140 million women and girls are estimated to have undergone FGC between the time they were babies and 16 years old. A further two million girls are considered to be at risk. Most live in Africa, although some are in Asia and the Middle East. They are also increasingly found in Europe, Australia, Canada and the US, mainly among immigrants from these countries.[11]

FGC is sometimes referred to as 'female circumcision', and involves 'partial or total removal of the external female genitalia or other injury to the female genital organs whether for cultural, religious or other non-therapeutic reasons'.[12] It is often performed without anesthetic and with unsterilized instruments.

Female genital cutting is claimed by some Muslims to be an Islamic practice, but in fact it predates Islam and is also practiced by followers of other religious beliefs. Its proponents argue that it is cleaner and healthier, and that it prevents women from being 'promiscuous' and therefore is necessary for a good marriage. In some places it is considered part of cultural heritage. Girls who do not have the operation may find themselves unable to marry and their whole family ostracized.

FGC can have severe health consequences. The

When saying 'I do' means saying 'I don't'

At their wedding in Durame, capital of Kembata district in Ethiopia, Genet Girma wore a placard around her neck which declared: 'I am not circumcised, learn from me.'

The bridegroom, Adissie Abossie, carried one which read: 'I am proud to marry an uncircumcised woman.'

Just how brave Girma and Abossie were in deciding to celebrate their marriage by taking a public stand against the practice of female genital cutting (FGC) is hard to appreciate without some idea of how widespread the practice is. Ninety per cent of women in Ethiopia have had the operation.

But attitudes to FGC in Ethiopia and elsewhere are slowly changing due to governmental and non-governmental interventions. The Kembata Women's Self-Help Centre (KMG), for instance, has been quietly working to eradicate FGC since 1997 by educating young girls and their families about its dangers.

Its school and community-based workshops and individual follow-ups have led some 4,000 women and girls to sign a pledge against FGC – and Girma was one of them.

'The reason I was able to avoid being circumcised is because of the training I took through KMG,' says Girma, who persuaded her parents to delay the procedure. Another incentive was her fiancé's strong opposition. 'He told me that if I am circumcised he wouldn't marry me,' she adds.

Abossie knew from personal experience the suffering FGC causes. 'I was the first child and I could see how difficult [subsequent] deliveries were for my mother,' he explains. 'Women who have experienced the most extreme form of FGC must be cut open and resewn after every birth. After I understood that it resulted from circumcision, I decided not to marry a circumcised girl.'

Other couples have now taken the same decision: KMG founder Dr Bogalech Gebre is thrilled, saying: 'Every [anti-FGC] wedding is becoming a forum for education,' while noting that 'change must come from within'.

Gebre, who was cut at the age of six, said: 'I understood the purpose [of] female genital excision was to excise my mind, excise my ability to live with all my senses intact.'

One girl child most definitely not at risk is Girma's and Abossie's two-month-old daughter. She is called Wimma, which means full or complete. ■

Abinet Aseffa

Panos features, www.panos.org.uk

operation is often performed with crude tools. Immediate complications include severe pain, shock, hemorrhage, urine retention, ulceration of the genital region and injury to adjacent tissue. Hemorrhage and infection can cause death. There is concern about possible HIV transmission. Other long-term consequences include cysts and abscesses, scar formation, urinary incontinence, painful sexual intercourse, sexual dysfunction and difficulties with childbirth.

At a conference on zero tolerance of FGC in Addis Ababa in February 2002, one speaker defined the practice as 'the scourge of Africa'.

Change is slow and difficult. In Eritrea over half the population opposes the practice – with slightly more than half the men and slightly less than half the women registering disapproval.

There have been other success stories. A number of African countries, including Burkina Faso, Central African Republic, Djibouti, Ghana, Guinea-Conakry and Senegal have now outlawed female genital cutting. In two regions in Chad, girls born in the 1980s were only half as likely to undergo FGC as girls born in the 1960s. But, in practice, traditional customs often prevail and progress is slow. In other countries there is evidence that its incidence is creeping slowly up again, as it is viewed as part of religious practice. In Egypt it has risen by 0.3 per cent to 97.3 per cent, in Sudan it has increased by one per cent to 90 per cent and in Côte d'Ivoire it is up almost two per cent to 44.5 per cent.[13]

Violence in conflict situations

The 20th century was the most violent in history. Nearly 110 million people died as the result of conflict and war; 310,000 people were killed in wars in 2000 alone. Sixty per cent of these were civilians. For every person killed directly in a conflict, nine more are likely to die of starvation or disease.

'Women are in double jeopardy...' say Amnesty International. 'Few countries treat their women as well as their men... While women are under-represented in national and international decision-making structures, they are over-represented among the victims of human-rights abuse.[14]

Conflict-related deaths

The 20th century has seen an unprecedented rise in the number of people dying in wars – increasing numbers of these are civilians and the majority are now women and children.

Century	Estimated deaths in war worldwide (millions)
16th	1.6
17th	6.1
18th	7.0
19th	19.4
20th	109.7

World Report on Violence and Health, WHO, 2002.

And women are the new victims of this escalation. Where previously it was mainly soldiers who died, civilians are now deliberately targeted in large numbers – the proportion of civilians killed and wounded as a result of hostilities has risen from 5 per cent of casualties at the turn of the last century to 65 per cent during the Second World War and 90 per cent in more recent conflicts. Women and children make up the majority of civilian casualties. They also make up 50 per cent of refugees.

Women experience the horrors of war in different ways from men. They too face death, mostly as non-combatants, but they also suffer sexual violence, rape and resultant pregnancy, abduction and slavery. At the same time they are responsible for their families.

Marion, aged 17, from Sierra Leone, tells her story:

'My family and I were hiding in a room during an attack when a rebel broke in. My mother was asked to give one of her children up or else the entire family would be killed. My mother gave me up. The rebels took me with them, and on our way to their camp I was raped by seven of them. I was bleeding heavily and unable to walk any further. They threatened to kill me if I did not go with them. I was held by them for one year. After I escaped, I asked myself: "Who will help me now"?'[15]

Deliberate targets

The deliberate infection of women with HIV/AIDS has given a new twist to the spread of the pandemic. Women have been intended targets in other ways as well; the use of brutal mass rape is an increasingly common tactic in modern warfare – often with the purpose of making them pregnant with the rapist's child as a form of ethnic domination.

Victims of war

From 1990 to 2000, girls under 18 were involved in armed conflicts in at least 39 countries; in 65 per cent of those countries there are documented cases of kidnapping and physical force being used to recruit girls.

- Estimates of the number of women raped during the war in Bosnia and Herzegovina between 1992 and 1995 vary between 10,000 and 60,000.
- Genocide in Rwanda left an estimated 65,000 households headed by children – 90 per cent of whom were girls. It is estimated that 250,000 women were exposed to sexual violence. More than 5,000 women were impregnated through rape. Many are now raising children fathered by men who killed their families.
- A 1997 survey of Burundian refugees in Tanzania found that over 25 per cent of the women in the camp of Kanembwa had faced some sort of violence.
- Rape was used as a weapon of war by all sides in the Democratic Republic of Congo in 1998.
- 94 per cent of displaced households in Sierra Leone had experienced sexual assaults, including rape, torture and sexual slavery. ∎

Women, war and peace, 2002, www.unifem.org; *World Report on Violence and Health*, WHO, 2002, www.who.org

---

The then UN Secretary-General, Boutros-Ghali, told the Beijing Conference that more women were suffering directly from the effects of war and conflict than ever before in history. 'There is a deplorable trend towards the organized humiliation of women, includ-

Violence in Gujarat

After the anti-Muslim violence in Gujarat, India, in early 2002, a women's fact-finding team went to investigate the extent of sexual violence. Their report reveals an horrific story of the rape and murder by Hindu gangs of countless Muslim women and girls. The majority were burned to death after they had been raped. The team's findings noted that the sexual violence was not carried out at random, but that there was 'pre-planning, organization, and precision in the targeting'. The State and the police were complicit. Few perpetrators have been brought to trial.

This is a short extract from their report.

Naroda Patia, Ahmedabad, 28 February 2002:

'The mob started chasing us with burning tires after we were forced to leave Gangotri society. It was then that they raped many girls. We saw about 8 to 10 rapes. We saw them strip 16-year-old Mehrunissa. They were stripping themselves and beckoning to the girls. Then they raped them right there on the road. We saw a girl's vagina being slit open. Then they were burnt. Now there is no evidence.'

'I saw Farzana being raped by Guddu Chara. Farzana was about 13 years old. She was a resident of Hussain Nagar. They put a *saria* (rod) in Farzana's stomach. She was later burnt. Twelve-year-old Noorjahan was also raped. The rapists were Guddu, Suresh and Naresh Chara and Haria. I also saw Bhawani Singh, who works in the State Transport Department, kill five men and a boy.'

'The mob, which came from Chara Nagar and Kuber Nagar, started burning people at around six in the evening. The mob stripped all the girls of the locality, including my 22-year-old daughter, and raped them. My daughter was engaged to be married. Seven members of my family were burnt including my wife (aged 40), my sons (aged 18, 14 and 7) and my daughters (aged 2, 4 and 22). My eldest daughter... died of 80-per-cent burn injuries.' ∎

How has the Gujarat Massacre affected minority women? The survivors speak. Fact-finding by a women's panel, April 2002.

ing the crime of mass rape,' he said. 'We will press for international legal action against those who perpetrate organized violence against women in time of conflict.'

Women's bodies have become part of the battlefield.

Ethnic and religious violence has meant that Muslim women in particular have been attacked simply because they are Muslim. The rape and murder of women during the anti-Muslim violence in Gujarat, India, is just one horrific example.

Legal successes

There have been a number of historic legal successes in the last few years for women who have suffered during war.

First, the designation of rape and enslavement as crimes against humanity. On 22 February 2001 the International Criminal Tribunal for the former Yugoslavia (ICTY) convicted Dragoljub Kunarac, Radomir Kovac and Zoran Vukovic for rape, torture and enslavement. It was an historic moment for women's rights – the first time in history that an international tribunal had convicted on the basis of crimes of sexual violence against women.

Regan Ralph, Director of the Women's Rights Division of Human Rights Watch, said: 'Finally, the international community is taking these sexual crimes – rapes, gang rapes and sexual enslavement of women – seriously. This interpretation will serve as the basis to prosecute others who enslave women around the world.' [16]

Second, the establishment of the International Criminal Court in July 2002, though marred by American refusal to take part, was another victory for women's rights activists. Rape, sexual slavery, enforced prostitution, forced pregnancy, enforced sterilization, sexual violence, and persecution on account of gender were defined in the ICC statutes as war crimes and crimes against humanity. The ICC Rules offer important protections for victims and witnesses, particularly those who suffer sexual or gender violence. Six of the top seven judges on the new International Criminal Court are women. 'It's completely historic,' said Vahida Nainar, of the Women's Caucus for Gender Justice. 'It's the first time for international courts. In 85 years the International Court of Justice has had just one woman judge.'[17]

Third, the establishment of a Women's International War Crimes Tribunal 2000, which sat in December of that year in Tokyo, Japan. Run by non-governmental organizations, this was established to

---

The Women's Millennium Peace Prize

Only about 10 per cent of Nobel Peace Prize winners have been women – the latest being Shirin Ebadi from Iran (see Chapter 1). The Women's Millennium Peace Prize awarded by the UN Fund for Women (UNIFEM) and International Alert, is given every three years. The first awards in 2001 went to four women and three organizations:

- *Ruta Pacífica de las Mujeres* (Women's Road to Peace), a Colombian group that has organized protests against violence throughout their country and arranged meetings between warring factions. In one meeting, unarmed women confronted guerrillas and placed carnations in their rifle barrels.
- *Leitana Nehan Women's Development Agency*, a Papua New Guinean group, for its cross-community work for peace during and after the nine-year war between Bougainville rebels and the PNG military.
- *Women in Black*, an international organization that protests against aggression and violence.
- *Dr Flora Brovina*, the Kosovar Albanian humanitarian, peace and human-rights campaigner imprisoned in 1999 by Serbian authorities.
- A posthumous award presented to *Veneranda Nzambazamariya*, the leader of Rwanda's women's movement, who helped rebuild the country after the genocide of 1994 and died in a plane crash in January 2000.
- *Asma Jahangir* and *Hina Jilani*, two sisters who for 20 years have risked their lives in defence of women and minorities in Pakistan. ■

---

consider the criminal liability of leading high-ranking Japanese military and political officials, and the separate responsibility of the State of Japan, for rape and sexual slavery arising out of Japanese military activity in the Asia Pacific region in the 1930s and 1940s. It had been a long time in the making, and many of the elderly women making submissions had never talked about their suffering before.

Fourth, the Truth and Reconciliation Commissions. In the last 15 years there have been 24 such commissions. Truth commissions are: 'Bodies established to research and report on human-rights abuses over a certain period of time in a particular country or in relation to a particular conflict.' The most famous is probably the one that was set up in South Africa to investigate abuses under apartheid, where many women testified.[18] In Sierra Leone, where a commission was established in 2000, the abuse of women's human rights was specifically singled out.

The Women's Millennium Peace Prize formally recognized the widespread and significant involvement

---

Young women protest in Cairo

On Friday 4 April 2003, 18-year-old Manar Ahmed was arrested along with approximately 50 other activists heading for Al-Sayeda Aisha Square, where an anti-war rally was supposed to take place.

'I have always asked myself what I would do if I were arrested. How would I react?' recounted Ahmed, who during the past two years has participated in several rallies along with her family, who are also politically active.

Ahmed's first reaction when detained by the police was fear. 'I was scared when they arrested me and separated me from my friends, my mother and brother. But when they led me to the police van filled with people I knew who had also been arrested, I relaxed. People were chanting anti-war slogans and I was not afraid anymore,' said Ahmed.

Ahmed looks back at her incarceration as a positive experience. 'I learned how to face a situation of which I had always been scared. I did not cry or freak out. I was strong and dealt with it.' ∎

of women in the peace movement. There are many women's peace groups, and some have a long history. The International Congress of Women goes back to World War One, when women from 12 countries braved the war to meet and discuss how to end the carnage. This group eventually became the Women's International League for Peace and Freedom, which now has branches throughout the world.

In 1988 women in Israel gathered to stand silently on the street to protest against their country's occupation of the West Bank and Gaza and to show their solidarity with Palestinian women. They stood at the same time each week, each day, silent and dressed all in black. Sometimes they were insulted and abused; sometimes people came to shake their hands. They were followed by women in many countries of the world and today Women in Black groups exist not only in Israel but all over the world.[19]

In 2003, women were at the forefront of anti-war marches, when over 30 million people around the world showed their objection to the US and Britain's war against Iraq.

The woman who has awoken

I'm the woman who has awoken
I've arisen and become a tempest through the ashes of
    my burnt children
I've arisen from the rivulets of my brother's blood
My nation's wrath has empowered me
My ruined and burnt villages fill me with hatred against
    the enemy,
I'm the woman who has awoken.

Part of a poem by Meena, founder of Rawa, Revolutionary Association of the Women of Afghanistan, born 1956, killed 1987. ■

http://rawa.fancymarketing.net/poems.htm

Double jeopardy

1 Joni Seager, *The Atlas of Women: an economic, social and political survey*, third edition, The Women's Press, 2003. **2** Judith Mirsky, *Beyond victims and villains; addressing sexual violence in the education sector*, Panos Institute, 2003. **3** Dialogue with refugee women, 20-22 June 2001, UNHCR. **4** UNIFEM. **5** United Nations Department of Public Information DPI/1772/HR, February 1996. **6** www.femnet.org **7** Women, War and Peace, UNIFEM, 2002. **8** United Nations Department of Public Information DPI/1772/HR, February 1996. **9** www.whiteribbon.ca **10** www.whiteribbon.ca **11** www.who.int/inf-fs/en/fact241.html **12** WHO definition. **13** http://www.unicef.org/exspeeches/2003/03esp07fgm.htm **14** March 1995 (AI Index: ACT 77/01/95). **15** Conference on Sexual and Gender-based violence, Geneva, 27-29 March 2001, UNHCR. **16** http://www.hrw.org/press/2001/02/serbia0222.htm **17** Chris Stephen, *The Observer*, 9 February 2003. **18** www.doj.gov.za/trc/hrvtrans/index.htm **19** www.womeninblack.net

9 Sexuality, relationships and old age

Relationships are changing. One in four households is now headed by a woman. But the majority of women still live under the control of their husbands. And for those who do not conform, life can be hard.

'In the old days we [women] were limited to the kitchen and never dared to leave the house. We spent the whole day grinding grain and doing other house chores. When our husbands came home they demanded that we wash their feet.'

Azenu, 45, farmer and female head of household, Ethiopia[1]

The changing state of marriage

FAMILIES ARE CHANGING. And so are relationships between men and women. Households are getting smaller and more are headed by a woman. In the North, fewer people are getting married – out-of-marriage births have increased more than 50 per cent in the last 20 years.[2]

While most women still spend the majority of their lives married, divorce is also on the increase – in Belarus, Russia, Sweden, Latvia and Ukraine there are more divorces than there are marriages.

Other things have changed very little. Women are still marrying much younger than men – in Nigeria 70 per cent of girls are married by the age of 19 but only 4 per cent of boys. In Honduras 30 per cent of girls are married by 19 but only 7 per cent of boys.

In many countries married women still 'belong' to their husbands and in some they need their husband's permission to buy or sell property, have an abortion, work, travel or open a bank account. In Swaziland married women are still legal minors, though under civil law they can sign a prenuptial agreement which gives them adult status. In Yemen the law says that a woman must obey her husband, live with him where he wants to live and not leave the home without his permission. In Kyrgyzstan the law prohibits divorce during pregnancy and while a child is less than a year old. In the north of Nigeria women can be flogged or stoned to death for adultery. Men all over the world are still beating their wives – and getting away with it.

Amina Lawal

On 22 March 2002 a Shari'a court in Katsina State, northern Nigeria, sentenced Amina Lawal to death after she confessed to having had a child while divorced. The man named as the father of her baby girl reportedly denied having sex with her and the charges against him were discontinued. Amina Lawal did not have a lawyer during her first trial, when the judgment was passed. But she filed an appeal against her sentence with the help of a lawyer hired by a Nigerian women's rights group.

On 19 August 2002 a Shari'a court of appeal upheld the sentence of death by stoning.

'The legal system is being used to punish adult women for consensual sex,' said LaShawn R Jefferson, executive director of the Women's Rights Division of Human Rights Watch. 'The death penalty is never an appropriate punishment for a crime and, in this instance, the very nature of the crime is in doubt.' There was no question of prosecuting the man.

On 25 September 2003 the Shari'a Court of Appeal quashed her sentence. According to her defense lawyer she was freed on the grounds that neither the conviction nor the confession were legally valid. Therefore no offence as such was established.

'Amina Lawal's case should not have been brought to a court of law in the first instance. Nobody should ever be made to go through a similar ordeal,' said Amnesty International. ■

www.amnesty.org

In other parts of the world the nature of marriage is beginning to change and legislation that gives women more rights within marriage is being pushed through.

Sharing the burden at home

While more women than ever before are working, men have still been reluctant to enter the domestic sphere and share in tasks like housework and childcare. In the US in 1965 men spent 12 hours a week cooking, cleaning and doing other housework, compared with 16 hours today – an extra hour per decade. In Sweden men do 23 hours, women 33; in Japan men do 6 hours, women 29.[3]

Elsewhere, research shows that between 2 and 12 per cent of men now do an equal share of housework. In South Asia women spend three to five hours more than men each week on subsistence activities such as carrying water and wood, and between 20 and 30 hours more on housework.

In the 1990s Australia became the first country to attempt to quantify this unpaid work; the calculations suggest that its value is equivalent to 58 per cent of Gross Domestic Product.[4]

Psychologists Claire Rabin and Pepper Schwartz found that when wives and husbands make what they both feel is a successful effort to divide chores fairly, both spouses benefit.[5] Inequities in housework and childcare have profound consequences for the marital satisfaction of women, which in turn affects the quality of the marriage for the man as well.

Equality often goes out the window once a couple have children. Says British political commentator Polly Toynbee: 'Young women outshining boys at school have a habit of thinking all the great feminist causes are won: but once they become mothers and are shocked to find it isn't so, they are too exhausted to do anything about it.' [6]

Lack of childcare is still a big problem throughout most of the Western world. Although grandmothers often help with childcare, it is mainly the responsibility of the parents, and usually the mother. Yet school days and work days rarely coincide, and state nursery provision is very patchy.

This may well become a problem for men as well. Men are still seen as the main breadwinners, and many are working longer rather than shorter days, leading to conflict with family needs. It is not just high-profile women who leave their jobs to 'be with their families' these days, but high-profile men as well. In New York City the proportion of men reporting significant conflict between work and family increased from 12 per cent in 1977 to 71 per cent in 1989.[7]

There has been a revolution for women in the workplace; now there needs to be a revolution which embraces both men and women at home.

Men and women

It seems that while women have changed a lot, men's behavior patterns towards women have changed very little. Susan Faludi, American author of *Backlash: the war against women*, believes that improvements in women's lives are dependent not just on women themselves but on men changing the way they behave: 'I would hope that men could grapple with the true nature of their burden and see that it's shared by women, and that men and women could find common ground to fight the forces that demean them both.'[8] Recognizing that entrenched attitudes begin at a young age, there are many projects working with young men as well as young women to help them look at their attitudes towards relationships.

In Brazil, 'male involvement in reproductive health and child care is limited; men generally feel that they are entitled to sex from women; tolerance of violence against women is fairly widespread.' So one project identified what factors were seen as 'gender equitable' and then held group discussions about life histories to help the young men see the 'costs' of traditional masculinities. And the Guy to Guy project has developed an award-winning play based in schools, to help young men change attitudes and behaviors and develop healthy relationships with women.[9]

In South Africa and Nicaragua similar projects with young men encourage them to examine and change traditional male behaviors. The HIV/AIDS epidemic has brought a new urgency to the need to encourage young men to practice safe sexual behavior – part of this is having more equitable relationships with women. Because young people's peer groups are a major influence, there is a wide range of peer-education projects, media-awareness campaigns and other initiatives like youth and sports clubs. A young man in Portugal, after one such program, noted that: 'There are certain rights that are fundamental. Sexual and reproductive rights are one of those. The attitude we should adopt concerning sexual and reproductive rights is to be conscious and responsible so we can make those rights a reality. That's our obligation. When I say OUR, I mean both men and women.'[10]

Sex education is fundamental here. In the Netherlands, where sex education starts early and focuses on relationships as much as on sex itself, the country has one of the lowest rates of teenage pregnancy in Europe; 56 per cent of young men cited 'love and commitment' as a reason for their first sexual intercourse. Researchers noted that 'since initial sex was more likely to occur within an emotional relationship, it was highly likely that there was… respect for the other's wishes.' Seventy-eight per cent of young men thought about pregnancy and 40 per cent were likely to talk about it with their partners. This compares with 57 per cent and 15 per cent in Britain, which has the highest rate of teenage pregnancy in Europe.[11]

Gay rights are women's rights

'Lesbian, gay, bisexual and transgender people have been vilified by presidents and political leaders, which has led to a culture of intolerance,' says Paula Ettelbrick, executive director of the International Gay and Lesbian Human Rights Commission. 'These attacks are just the first step in creating a climate in which all rights are at risk.'[12]

Around two per cent of the world's women live exclusively as homosexuals. Many more are forced to keep their sexuality secret. In 70 countries being homosexual is illegal and in seven Muslim countries it can mean life imprisonment or even execution. Members of the Bush Administration in the US also hold anti-gay views. Right-wing Senator Rick Santorum said: 'If the Supreme Court says that you have the right to consensual (gay) sex within your home, then you have the right to bigamy, you have the right to polygamy, you have the right to incest, you have the right to adultery. You have the right to anything.'

The American Christian Right has an active lobby against what it sees as 'immoral and irrational' practices. Gary De Mar, from American Vision, an organization 'Dedicated to Restoring America's Biblical Foundations', asks: 'Does it ever register with homosexuals that maybe God is telling them something when they get life-threatening diseases because of their sexual practices and can have no children no matter how hard they try? Like Dr Frankenstein, homosexuals take God's design of marriage and manufacture an artificial monster from its parts.'[13]

In some parts of the West, attitudes to homosexuality have become more tolerant.

'There has been a grassroots revolution in the past 15 to 20 years,' says Jeffrey Weeks, Professor of Sociology at London South Bank University and a leading authority on the history of gay and lesbian sexuality. 'We are living in a much more secular society. People no longer believe that the church should lay down the law on sexual behavior, and we rely far more on our own decision-making.' Britain is generally becoming more open, he adds. 'More lesbians and gays are coming out, more people are co-habiting, there are more single parents, so it's simply not possible to be moralistic about the things that we used to be. Everyone now knows someone who would have been regarded as deviant a few decades ago.' Public opinion has meant pressure on government and has led to legislation that allows gay and lesbian partners to register their relationships as 'civil partnerships' and transsexuals to be issued with new birth certificates.[14]

But similarly, repressive attitudes towards homosexuality are matched by repressive laws about women's rights in general, as in Saudi Arabia, where women are severely restricted and homosexuality can be punished by death. This connection has long been recognized by feminists; at the first international Women's Conference in 1985 in Nairobi, lesbians from the South released the following statement: 'The struggle for lesbian rights is indispensable to any

---

'I don't believe they [lesbians and homosexuals] have any rights at all.'

Zimbabwean president Robert Mugabe, 2 August 1995.

struggle for basic human rights. It's part of the struggle for all women for control over our own lives.'[15] One Zimbabwean woman asked: 'How can we expect our black lesbian sisters to find their voice in our society when they cannot even speak for themselves within their own families?... Gay liberation is integral to the fight against racism and gender oppression. As long as women are not free, then lesbians are not free.'[16]

Ageing

By 2020 there will be more than a billion people aged 60 and over. More than 700 million of these will be living in the countries of the South. A large proportion will be women because, in general, women still live longer than men and women's life expectancy has gone up. In 1992 the average woman lived to be 62.9 years in developing countries compared to 53.7 years in 1970. In industrialized countries women's average life expectancy in 1992 was 79.4 years, up from 74.2 in 1970. In 23 countries women had a life expectancy of

Female life expectancy at birth 2000

Female life expectancy has been increasing in many countries, but in others it is going down. A woman in Japan can expect to live to 84, while a woman in Malawi may not even see her fortieth birthday.

Top ten		Bottom ten	
1 Japan	84.4	136 Uganda	44.6
2 France	82.4	137 Djibouti	44.2
2 Hong Kong	82.4	138 Zimbabwe	42.5
4 Sweden	82.2	139 Burundi	41.4
5 Switzerland	82.1	141 Rwanda	40.9
6 Spain	82.0	141 Zambia	40.9
7 Italy	81.5	143 Mozambique	40.2
8 Norway	81.5	143 Sierra Leone	40.2
8 Canada	81.5	144 Botswana	40.1
8 Belgium	81.5	145 Malawi	39.8

over 80 in 2000. At the bottom end of the scale, women in Sierra Leone can only expect to live to 40.2 years and men 37.6.[17]

This 'gray revolution' will have an enormous effect on women, families and relationships. The largest increases in older populations have been occurring in Asia and Africa. By 2025 the proportion of women aged 60 or over will almost double in East and Southeast Asia, Latin America and the Caribbean, and North Africa. Women are more likely to be widowed. In some countries, traditional widowhood practices can result in abuse and even violence. Widows have often spent long years caring for their husbands – before then for their parents, afterwards for their grandchildren. Grandmothers are often the main source of childcare in a world where the majority of women work. This is particularly true when one or both parents have to migrate in search of work, and in countries where large numbers of parents die of AIDS. And yet women in older age are often neglected both by analysts and policy makers. Given the changing demography across the world, this is likely to become an increasingly important issue.

1 www.mountainvoices.org **2** All the following information from Joni Seager, *The Atlas of Women*, The Women's Press, 2003. **3** www.umich.edu **4** Australian Bureau of Statistics, 1994. **5** http://www.positive-way.com/men,.htm **6** 'The mother of all issues' in *The Guardian*, 6 June 2003. **7** *Men and their Children*, Institute for Public Policy Research, London 1996. **8** *Mother Jones*, interview with Susan Faludi by Susan Halpern, September/October 1999. **9** Judy Mirsky, *Beyond victims and villains: addressing sexual violence in the education sector*, Panos, 2003. **10** www.ippf.org/resource/index.htm **11** Judy Mirsky, *Beyond victims and villains: addressing sexual violence in the education sector*, Panos, 2003. **12** http://hrw.org/press/2003/05/safrica051403.htm **13** http://www.americanvision.org/ **14** *The Guardian*, 12 December 2003. **15** R Rosenbloom (ed), *Unspoken Rules: sexual orientation and women's human rights*, Cassell, 1996. **16** www.amnesty.org **17** Human development index, *Human Development Report 2002*, UNDP.

10 Organized women

Much of this book has shown how so many women still live in situations of great hardship and oppression. But the strides forward that they have made were achieved as a result of thousands of women's groups and organizations around the world refusing to give up the struggle for a better world for all.

'We are the ones who first ploughed the earth when Modise (God) made it. We are the ones who make the food. We are the ones who look after the men when they are little boys, when they are young men, and when they are old and about to die. We are always there. But we are just women, and nobody sees us.'

An old Setswana poem[1]

Women's voices were heard loudly during the 1990s, when international conferences made sure that women were in the public eye. Six thousand women attended the first UN women's conference in Mexico in 1985; 30,000 went to Beijing in 1995. And these were only a fraction of the women who had been organizing – in microcredit groups, against violence, for women's right to choose, for changes in the law, to save their environment, for better pay and conditions, to ensure that 'women's rights are human rights'.

There have been many successes during the last few years; successes that have benefited both sexes. Homosexuality is less persecuted, at least in the urban West. Women in the Anglican Church are now allowed to become vicars (priests) and even bishops. Several countries have banned female circumcision. Many have passed laws banning discrimination in the workplace. Women have been appointed all over the world (though still in small numbers) as parliamentarians, judges and top executives. There has been a sea change in many countries in the way women are

International Women's Day: the Global Women's Strike

For the last three years, 8 March, International Women's Day, has not only been marked by activities across the world, but by a women's strike, calling for a 'total change of priorities'.

The Global Women's Strike is an independent and international network of grassroots women in 61 countries: '$800 billion a year is spent on military budgets worldwide, less than $20 billion is spent on all the essentials of life – accessible clean water, health, sanitation, basic education. Women make the world go round, and raise and look after its entire population; but at least two-thirds of the work we do is unwaged and unvalued – even though it's worth at least $11 trillion a year. Because of racism, Black and immigrant women work even harder, and in countries with the least resources the burden of women's and girls' work is most crushing. This basic sexist injustice devalues women and everything women do. It keeps our wages 25 per cent to 50 per cent below men's. In fact, though a few women are now highly paid, the gap between women's and men's wages is growing.'

The Global Women's Strike demands:

- The abolition of 'Third World debt'. Women in the South are owed billions for centuries of work.
- Accessible clean drinking water and ecologically sound appropriate technology for every household.
- Affordable, and accessible, housing and transport.
- Protection against violence – at home, in factory or office, on the farm, on the street.
- Pay equity for all – equal pay for work of equal value – internationally.
- Decent wages for caring work, whether in the family or outside.
- Paid maternity leave and breastfeeding breaks at paid employment.
- Increased pensions, child benefit and other benefits paid to mothers and other carers.
- Implementation of the UN decision (Beijing 1995) to measure and value the unwaged work done by women and men in national economic statistics.

http://womenstrike8m.server101.com/index.html

viewed. The younger generation of Western women, though they may not acknowledge it, have benefited from the battles fought by their mothers.

Changing times

From the small to the sweeping, there have been changes since 2000 that have improved women's lives in many countries.

Malaysia 2000 Women lawyers allowed to wear trousers in court.
Brazil 2001 Changes to the Civil Code grant equal rights to women in marriage and divorce, in household decision-making authority, and a wide range of family matters.
Netherlands 2001 Gay and lesbian marriages granted full recognition on equal terms with heterosexual marriages.
Pakistan 2001 A women-only post office opens in Karachi.
Turkey 2001 Parliament revises the Civil Code to recognize women's equality. Women no longer need their husbands' permission to work outside the home. Married women enjoy property rights and are allowed to keep their maiden name after marriage.
Britain 2001 The "morning-after" contraceptive pill becomes available without prescription for women over 16.
Bahrain 2002 Women allowed to vote and run for all elected offices.
Iran 2002 Parliament approves a bill granting women the right to seek a divorce in court.
Lithuania 2002 The government repeals a requirement that women undergo a gynecological examination to qualify for a driver's license.
Norway 2002 Government orders companies to ensure that at least 40 per cent of the board members are women.
Vietnam 2002 Government bans polygamy and dowries in marriage.

Joni Seager, *Atlas of Women*, Women's Press, 2003.

In the beginning, women marched alone and organized as women's groups. But, increasingly, they have been joined by men who see that change in favor of women will benefit both sexes. Men like those from the White Ribbon campaign against violence against women, or the increasing numbers who take time off from work to look after their children, or like Adisse Abossie, who take a stand against practices like female genital cutting (see chapter 8).

It is easy to forget just how recently so many women's rights have been won; and how many women still face violations of their rights on a daily basis. Charting the changes for the better, but remembering how hard-won they have been, is a crucial part of holding back the tide that threatens, little by little, to sweep many of these achievements away.

> You may write me down in history
> With your bitter, twisted lies,
> You may tread me in the very dirt
> But still, like dust, I'll rise.
> You may shoot me with your words,
> You may cut me with your eyes,
> You may kill me with your hatefulness,
> But still, like air, I'll rise.
> Out of the huts of history's shame
> I rise
> Up from a past that's rooted in pain
> I rise
> I'm a black ocean, leaping and wide,
> Welling and swelling I bear in the tide.
> Leaving behind nights of terror and fear
> I rise
> Into a daybreak that's wondrously clear
> I rise
> Bringing the gifts that my ancestors gave,
> I am the dream and the hope of the slave.
> I rise
> I rise
> I rise.

Maya Angelou

1 Alexander McCall Smith, *The No 1 Ladies' Detective Agency*, Abacus 2003.

The end – and the beginning

I WANT TO end near what was, for me, the beginning. My own initiation into feminism and the Women's Liberation Movement started at college, and grew steadily during the year I spent in India.

I still remember a story told to me by the *adivasi* (tribal) women who lived in the forests around the village where I stayed in Maharashtra. The community had started to brew illegal – and very strong – liquor and the men were getting drunk and beating up their wives. This was something that had not happened on this scale before, and the women did not know what to do about it. One day they got together and decided that every time they heard a woman being beaten they would all surround the couple until the husband was too embarrassed to continue. It worked. The abuse stopped. So did the brewing of liquor. And the men saw the benefits of better relationships as well. As one man said simply: 'Now I look at my wife and her eyes smile at me.'

Lynne Segal, one of the clearest thinkers during those early years, now a professor of psychology and gender studies, wrote recently that: 'The point of feminism is to say we need to change the way things are organized so that people don't feel alone.'

This was what the adivasi women in India had done. It was what feminism is all about – for women to be able to act together to combat the abuse of their rights and to build better relationships with their partners (male or female), their communities and the world.

The same spirit that inspired the feminist movement now inspires citizens' movements across the world, from the 30 million people who marched against the war on Iraq, to those who protest against globalization or the patenting of local seeds by transnational corporations.

The protesters are men and women, black and white, Christian and Muslim, old and young. They include some of those who can still remember the days when women had no vote. Ghada Razuki of Britain's Stop the War Coalition tells of an 80-year-old woman who phoned up wanting to help. 'But I'm afraid I am not very mobile,' she said. 'Never mind, I'll send you some leaflets and posters to give your friends,' said Ghada. 'No dear, you don't understand,' said the 80-year-old. 'I was planning to lie down on the motorway!'

They also include those like my 15-year old daughter who believes she is equal to any boy – and sometimes better. Hooked on shopping, she is nonetheless steeped in feminist principles, even if she does not call herself a feminist.

Is feminism dead? Long live feminism!

Contacts

These are just a few of the many groups that exist to support women's rights and work on gender issues. Not included are the thousands of local groups that have been so effective in bringing about change.

INTERNATIONAL
DAWN (Development Alternatives with Women for a New Era)
A Third World feminist network which looks at the cultural and economic factors related to women's participation in the development process. The DAWN Secretariat is based at:
PO Box 13124
Suva
Fiji
Tel/Fax: +679 314 770
Email: admin@dawn.org.fj
Website: www.dawn.org.fj

Human Rights Watch – Women's Rights Division
News, facts and articles on women's rights around the world. There are several offices in different countries. The main one is:
350 Fifth Avenue
34th floor
New York , NY 10118-3299
USA
Tel: +1 212 290 4700
Fax: +1 212 736 1300
Email: hrwnyc@hrw.org
Website: www.hrw.org/women

Amnesty International
Has regular updates on women's human rights at:
Website: www.amnesty.org

ISIS
Created in 1974 as an international channel of information and communication between women and now has connections in over 150 countries.
PO Box 1837
Quezon City Main
Philippines
Tel: +632 435 3405
Fax: +632 9241065
Website: www.isiswomen.org

UNIFEM (The United Nations Development Fund for Women)
Provides financial and technical assistance to programs and strategies that promote women's human rights, political participation and economic security.
304 E45th Street
15th Floor
New York, NY 10017
USA
Tel: +1 212 906 6400

Fax: +1 212 906 6705
Website: www.unifem.org

Women in Black
An international peace network. There are Women in Black groups all around the world. For details see:
Website: www.womeninblack.net

Women's International League for Peace and Freedom (WILPF)
Has branches and campaigns in most countries. Their central offices are at:
1 rue de Varembe
1211 Geneva 20
Switzerland
Tel: +41 22 919 7080
Fax: +41 22 919 7081
Email: wilpf@iprolink.ch
Website: www.wilpf.int.ch

AOTEAROA/NEW ZEALAND
National Council of Women of New Zealand (Inc)/Te Kaunihera Wahine o Aotearoa
With 38 branches throughout the country, the Council functions to serve women, the family and the community through discussion and action.
PO Box 12-117
10 Park Street
Thorndon
Wellington
Tel: +64 4 473 7623
Fax: +64 4 499 5554
Email: contactus@ncwnz.co.nz
Website: www.nzwnz.co.nz

AUSTRALIA
Ministry for the Status and Advancement of Women
Aims to improve the status of women in government, the commercial sector and other workplaces, undertake and provide research, consultation and education and promote service provision.
Level 11
100 William Street
Woolloomooloo
NSW 2011
Tel: +61 2 334 1160

BRITAIN
Gender and Development Network (GADN)
GADN in Britain is made up of over 130 gender practitioners, consultants and academics. It is the British platform for Women In Development Europe (WIDE), a Europe-wide network of gender and development professionals:
c/o WOMANKIND Worldwide
Viking House
32-37 Cowper Street
London EC2A 4AW

Contacts

Tel: +44 20 7549 5700
Email: brita@womankind.org.uk

Women Against Fundamentalisms
Committed to networking, challenging and organizing against manifestations of fundamentalism in all religions and to disseminate information about fundamentalist activities affecting women.
Email: nadje@gn.apc.org
Website: www.waf@gn.apc.org
Also

Women Living Under Muslim Laws
Email: wluml@mneet.fr
Website: www.wluml.org

Women's Environmental Network
Informs, educates and empowers women who care about the environment. Current campaigns include forest and paper, air pollution, the glamor industry and sanitary protection.
PO Box 30626
London E1 1TZ
Tel: +44 20 7481 9004
Fax: +44 20 7481 9144
Email:info@wen.org.uk
Website: www.wen.org.uk

CANADA
Women in the Americas
A new initiative to build links between women's groups in Canada and the South, especially around the impact of economic restructuring on women's lives.
c/o Oxfam Canada
294 Albert Street
Ste 300
Ottawa
ON K1P 6E6
Tel: +1 613 237 5236
Fax: +1 613 2370524

UNITED STATES
National Organization of Women
Campaigns and lobbies on major women's issues including equal rights, abortion and violence against women.
733 15th St NW
2nd floor
Washington, DC 20005
Tel: +1 202 628 8669
Fax: +1 202 785 8576
Email: now@now.org
Website: www.now.org

Third Wave Foundation
Young feminist activism for social change.
511 W 25th St
Suite 301
New York, NY 10001
Email: info@thirdwavefoundation.org
Tel: +1 212 675 0700
Fax: +1 212 255 6653
Email: 3Wave@nyo.com
Website: www.thirdwavefoundation.org

Women's Environment and Development Organization (WEDO)
Works to put women's issues on the UN agenda. Also supports development of an international network of women activists concerned with environment, development and social justice.
355 Lexington Avenue
3rd Floor
New York, NY 10017-6603
Tel: +1 212 973 0325
Fax: +1 212 9730335
E-mail: wedo@wedo.org
Website: www.wedo.org

Books and magazines

Again, this is just a small selection of the many relevant books.

Vanessa Baird, *The No-Nonsense Guide to Sexuality Diversity*, New Internationalist/Verso, 2001. A guide to the full range of issues worldwide.
Susan Faludi, *Backlash: the Undeclared War on Women*, Chatto and Windus, 1991. Still a classic.
Alissa Quart *Branded* Random House, 2003
Save the Children, *The State of the World's Mothers 2000*. Lots of information and statistics.
Joni Seager, *The Atlas of Women*, Women's Press, 2003. Detailed maps show what has changed and what has not.
Caroline Sweetman (ed), *Focus on Gender* series, Oxfam (www.oxfam.org.uk). A very useful series on a wide range of international issues, from globalization to climate change.
Trouble and Strife, 'the radical feminist magazine'. Appears twice a year. Well worth a read. 39 Eburne Road, London, N7 6AU, Britain.
UNIFEM, *The Progress of Women 2002*. A thorough look at all aspects of women's lives.
Natasha Walter, *The New Feminism*, Virago, 1999. A particular take on feminist issues.

Index

Bold page numbers refer to main
subjects of boxed text.

Index

Index